FSC
www.fsc.org
MIX
Papier aus verantwortungsvollen Quellen
Paper from responsible sources
FSC® C105338

Vimbai Lisa Michelle Jana

Adopting a Harmonized Regional Approach to Customs Regulation for the Tripartite Free Trade Agreement

Anchor Academic
Publishing

Jana, Vimbai Lisa Michelle: Adopting a Harmonized Regional Approach to Customs Regulation for the Tripartite Free Trade Agreement, Hamburg, Anchor Academic Publishing 2017

Buch-ISBN: 978-3-96067-190-9
PDF-eBook-ISBN: 978-3-96067-690-4
Druck/Herstellung: Anchor Academic Publishing, Hamburg, 2017

Bibliografische Information der Deutschen Nationalbibliothek:
Die Deutsche Nationalbibliothek verzeichnet diese Publikation in der Deutschen Nationalbibliografie; detaillierte bibliografische Daten sind im Internet über http://dnb.d-nb.de abrufbar.

Bibliographical Information of the German National Library:
The German National Library lists this publication in the German National Bibliography. Detailed bibliographic data can be found at: http://dnb.d-nb.de

Hermannstal 119k, 22119 Hamburg
http://www.diplomica-verlag.de, Hamburg 2017
Printed in Germany

DEDICATION

To my son Jordan, for giving me the strength to walk through the rain;
To my late father, Victor Lewis Jana for instilling in me the priceless value of an education;
To my mother Esther Jana, for shining like a beacon and leading by example;
To my sisters, Tsitsi and Tatenda for believing in me; and
To my aunts Senzeni and Netsai, thank you for being my pillars of support.
The joy of the Lord has truly been my strength.

ACKNOWLEDGEMENT

First, I would like to express my heartfelt gratitude to Professor Rieke Wandrag. Words are inadequate to fully express my gratitude to you for transforming my dreams to reality through enabling me to pursue this programme and affording me a once in a lifetime opportunity to reach for the stars.

Secondly, I would also like to thank my supervisor, Professor Patricia Lenaghan, who has been patient with me and has brought out the best within me. Thank you for constantly urging me to dig deep within myself to reach for excellence. I am also deeply grateful for the financial assistance given to me by the University of Western Cape and Australian Aid which funded my LLM studies.

Thirdly, I would like to thank my family, especially my mother and my sisters Tsitsi and Tatenda, for their unfaltering support, without which I could not have made it through with my studies. I am truly thankful for their positive voices, their endless encouragement, their prayers and much needed financial support. To my son, my sunshine Jordan, without realising it, you have been my inspiration to go on. The mere thought of you has strengthened my resolve to succeed.

Finally, I wish to thank my Lord, Jehovah Jireh, who has been faithful to me in all things and through all things, providing to me all sufficient grace.

KEYWORDS

Automated System for Customs Data
Costs of Trade
Customs
Customs Union of the European Union
Doha Development Agenda
Harmonisation of National Customs Procedures
Information and Communications Technology
One Stop Border Post
Regional Integration
Regional Customs and Trade Policy
Single Automated and Interoperable Electronic Customs System
Single Window
Trade Facilitation
Tripartite Free Trade Agreement

ACRONYMS AND ABBREVIATIONS

AACE	African Alliance for E-commerce
AEC	African Economic Community
ASEAN	Association of South East Asian Nations
ASYCUDA	Automated Systems for Customs Data
AU	African Union
CET	Common External Tariff
COMESA	Common Market for Eastern and Southern Africa
CU	Customs Union
CTTTFP	Comprehensive Tripartite Trade and Transport Facilitation Programme
DFID	Department for International Development
EAC	East African Community
EC	European Community
ECSC	European Coal and Steel Community
EEC	European Economic Community
EU	European Union
FTA	Free Trade Area
GATT	General Agreement on Tariffs and Trade
GDP	Gross Domestic Product
ICT	Information and Communications Technology
OAU	Organisation of African Union
OSBP	One Stop Border Post
PAA	Pan Asia E-Commerce Alliance
REC	Regional Economic Community
RISDP	Regional Indicative Strategic Development Plan
SEA	Single European Act
SAD	Single Administrative Document
SADC	Southern African Development Community
TFTA	Tripartite Free Trade Agreement
UN	United Nations
UNCTAD	United Nations Conference on Trade and Development
USAID	United States Agency for International Development
WCO	World Customs Organisation
WTO	World Trade Organisation

TABLE OF CONTENTS

CHAPTER ONE: INTRODUCTION AND OVERVIEW

1.1 BACKGROUND

The three regional economic communities (REC's) in Eastern and Southern Africa which are the Common Market for Eastern and Southern Africa (COMESA), the East African Community (EAC), and the Southern African Development Community (SADC) together have recognised the need to work towards regional cooperation aimed at the eventual creation of a single regional economic community or Tripartite Free Trade Agreement (TFTA) which will replace the existent REC's in Eastern and Southern Africa to which the member states of these two regions have multiple membership.[1] COMESA, EAC and SADC as the TFTA region ('the region') combined comprises a total of twenty seven member states which have a combined population of 527 million people, a combined gross domestic product (GDP) of USD624 billion.[2] These statistics translate into a potential regional economic powerhouse for Eastern and Southern Africa.[3]

One of the major goals of the TFTA is to harmonise trade arrangements among the three REC's, improve the movement of goods and persons within the single integrated region, facilitate the joint implementation of regional infrastructure projects and enhance co-operation of member states.[4] This is a laudable initiative by the member states of the three REC's and it is recognised that regional integration is the first step towards integration into a multilateral trading system. For the TFTA member states, it is crucial that there be an awareness and move towards a review of domestic customs legislation and policy and the development of regional supranational legislation and regulations in order to gain a stronger competitive edge in the global market.[5]

---

[1]COMESA-EAC-SADC Tripartite - institutional framework available at http://www.comesa-eac-TFTA-tripartite.org/home (accessed 4 May 2013).
[2]COMESA-EAC-SADC Tripartite – members and background information available at http://www.comesa-eac-TFTA-tripartite.org/members (accessed 4 May 2013).
[3]Mills G and E. Sidiropoulis *'Trends Problems and projections in Southern African Integration'* in Clapham C, Mills G, et al *'Regional Integration in South Africa: Comparative International Perspectives'* (2001) 2.
[4]TradeMark South Africa available at http://www.trademarksa.org/node/1042 (accessed 4 May 2013).
[5] Lamy P *'The challenge of integrating Africa into the World Economy''* In Clapham C, Mills G, et al *'Regional Integration In South Africa: Comparative International Perspectives'* (2001) 15.

While these aims may yet sound ambitious, the goals are indeed plausible and achievable.[6] The three REC's are now more than ever facing increased and unprecedented volumes of trade due to the general increase in trade volumes on a global level.[7] It is of vital importance that the TFTA be able to exercise flexibility and allow its trade facilitation policies to evolve in order to adapt and keep up with global trends in trade. The borders of the envisaged single regional economic community which will eventually replace COMESA, EAC and SADC must now more than ever, be efficient and allow for the quicker processing of goods as trade volumes into the region continuously increase.

In this singular spirit of regional economic development and integration, it becomes worthwhile to draw a few lessons and pointers from the Customs Union (CU) of the European Union (EU) which has over time, successfully managed to evolve to adapt to changing trends in international trade and customs processing to efficiently manage vastly increased cross-border movement of goods.[8] A single customs legislative framework for the TFTA can become a reality through the driving of fundamental reforms in the area of national customs policymaking and adapting domestic legislation to be developed to be harmonised at regional level which will effectively and vastly reduce the costs of trade, increasing trade volumes and minimising and simplifying bureaucratic processes at national borders and points of entry into the region.[9]

This process is no mean feat and will involve strong political willpower and cooperation from the member states and a certain degree of surrendering national sovereignty[10] as the development of a single automated and interoperable electronic customs system for the TFTA will be a project of mammoth proportions requiring dedicated financial commitment from all stakeholders involved.[11] This proposed introduction, development and maintenance of a

---

[6] Evans D 'Options for regional integration in Southern Africa' *IDS Working paper* 94. 5-8.

[7]WCO: 'There is strong commitment to customs modernisation in Africa' *All Africa.com* 14 March 2012 available at *http://allafrica.com/stories/201203141063.html* (accessed 4 May 2013).

[8]Maitland C and Van Gorp, 2009, 'Beyond Harmonization: ICT Policymaking in Regional Economic Communities', *Information Society*, 25, 1, 27.

[9]Messerlin P, Zarouk J, 'Trade Facilitation: Technical regulations and customs procedures', *World Economy* 23, (2000) Vol. 4 580-584.

[10] Clapham C '*The challenge of integrating Africa into the World Economy*'' In Clapham C, Mills G, et al '*Regional Integration In South Africa: Comparative International Perspectives*' (2001) 60.

[11]UNCTAD Trust Fund for trade facilitation negotiations technical note 13 available at *http://www.unctad.org/technicalnotes* (accessed 4 May 2013).

single automated and interoperable electronic customs system will allow for the exchange of information between customs offices within the region as a whole.

This mini-thesis shies away from proposing a 'quick fix' or 'instant benefit' to the harmonisation of TFTA member states customs legislative frameworks and policies and the development of a single automated and interoperable electronic customs system but rather places its focus on long-term sustainable benefits which will be realised over time. The harmonisation of TFTA member state customs legislative policies and the resultant Information and Communications Technology (ICT) reforms to the customs processes of the TFTA member states, though not immediate or short-term, will strategically position the region to conduct business in an increasingly volume driven, fast paced, electronic global economy.

This will in turn propel the TFTA as a regional economic block to realise greater economic successes in the long run. A single automated and interoperable electronic customs system will also cater for essential controls over customs duties and a common external tariff in a consistent transparent manner across the region[12]. Harmonisation of national customs policies and a common electronic customs system will be beneficial as it will provide vital information and statistics with regards to every movement of goods exported or imported from and into the TFTA.

With global trade volumes increasing phenomenally, customs processing technology will be a major driver of regional economic development and fundamental over-arching reforms will have to be undertaken in the realm of customs ICT, hardware and software in order to realise the real financial benefits of creating of a common customs area for the region. This will assist in the elimination of the duplication of customs processes.[13] A TFTA harmonised customs system on a legal and technological front will increase the competitiveness of businesses operating in the region, reduce wasteful costs of trade and improve regional customs controls.

---

[12]Wilson J, et al *'Assessing the Benefits of Trade Facilitation: A Global Perspective' The World Bank, Institute for International Economics, Washington DC, and Osaka University, Japan*

[13]UNCTAD Trust Fund for trade facilitation negotiations: technical note 13 available at *http://unctad.org/en/docs/TN13_DocumentSimplification.pdf* (accessed 4 May 2013).

In developing a regional customs legislative framework and policy, modernising the customs systems of member states and developing a common electronic customs system, it may be prudent to draw a few lessons from the CU of the EU which is one of the main pillars of the EU, and whose creation, development, modernisation and simplification of a customs legal and technological environment has taken place gradually over a period of several years beginning with an amendment to the European Community (EC) Customs Code.[14] This major amendment gave EU customs authorities the powers to implement some of the most advanced security requirements in the world, while creating an environment which did not disrupt or create blockages to legitimate trade.

The first step to the EU-wide electronic exchange of customs declarations was established with the inception of its computerised transit system which started in 1997. As a contribution to the 'e-government' programme, in July 2003, the EC Commission[15] published its communication on a paperless environment for customs and trade.[16] This official communication provided a vision of a modern customs service for all the EU member states communicating electronically. This vision was endorsed by the council resolution of December 5, 2003[17] which recognised the importance of a paperless environment for customs and trade, a common automated customs system and the inter-operability and exchange of electronic information between member states.

1.2 RESEARCH OBJECTIVES

Due to current existing disparities in customs legislation and procedural aspects at a member state level and the current move by the COMESA-EAC-SADC tripartite to work towards a unified economic community, it has become crucial to rethink nationalist customs policies

[14]EC Commission regulation 648/2005 of the European Parliament and of the Council amending Council Regulation (EEC) No 2913/92 ; EC Commission regulation 2913/92 of 12 October 1992 establishing the community customs available at http://eur-lex.europa.eu/LexUriServ/LexUriServ.do?uri=CELEX:32005R0648:en:HTML (accessed 4 May 2013).

[15]EC Commission regulation 2913/92 of 12 October 1992 establishing the community customs code available at http://eur-lex.europa.eu/LexUriServ/LexUriServ.do?uri=CELEX:31992R2913:en:HTML (accessed 4 May 2013).

[16]COM/2003/452 OF 24/07/2003 A simple and paperless environment for customs and trade available at http://ec.europa.eu/prelex/detail_dossier_real.cfm?CL=en&DosId=184452 (accessed 4 May 2013).

[17]EC Commission regulation 2286/2003 of 18 December 2003 available at http://eur-lex.europa.eu/LexUriServ/LexUriServ.do?uri=OJ:L:2003:343:0001:0123:en:PDF (accessed 4 May 2013).

and strategies in order to allow for the adoption a supranational approach to customs processes in order to realise the adoption of a single integrated regional approach to customs and trade facilitation for the TFTA.

Unless a change to supranational thinking is adopted, the costs of trade for the region can become significant and prohibitive for international traders and subsequently prove to be a deterrent to investors from conducting business in the region as a whole due to unforeseen and unpredictable costs and lack of familiarity with differing individual member state customs processes which vary significantly from jurisdiction to jurisdiction. It is therefore in the best interests of the TFTA region to formulate a simplified, single legal and technological framework for a coordinated approach towards the creation of a uniform set of customs laws and trade facilitation procedures which are easily accessible, adequately publicised in the public domain and well-known by traders.

Customs today, as a sub-component of trade facilitation efforts, finds itself firmly positioned at the interface of a rapidly dynamic global trading environment which is characterised by rapid consumption patterns, increased trade volumes, terrorism, organised crime, and modern hazards in the form of the movement of dangerous goods such as drug precursors.[18] The members of the TFTA, in harnessing their full combined economic potential through trade, must work together towards the harmonisation of their customs policies and develop a single customs legislative framework which is supranational and takes precedence over national domestic law. This is essential if the single integrated economic is to realise tangible and measurable trade benefits.[19]

1.3 <u>RESEARCH QUESTION</u>

In line with the above proposal, this mini-thesis puts forward the following questions:

[18] Southern Africa Regional Integration strategy paper 2011 – 2015 *African Development Bank* (2011) available at *http://www.afdb.org/fileadmin/uploads/afdb/Documents/Project-and-Operations/2011-2015%20-%20Southern%20Africa%20-%20Regional%20Integration%20Strategy%20Paper.pdf* (accessed 4 May 2013).

[19] Southern Africa Regional Integration strategy paper 2011 – 2015 *African Development Bank* *http://www.afdb.org/fileadmin/uploads/afdb/Documents/Project-and-Operations/2011-2015%20-%20Southern%20Africa%20-%20Regional%20Integration%20Strategy%20Paper.pdf* (accessed 4 May 2013).

a) Is harmonisation of the customs legislation and policies of the member states of the TFTA a necessity to achieve full regional integration and growth? and if so,
b) What are the benefits of harmonisation of regional customs systems in terms of a unified legislative and technological framework for the TFTA?
c) What challenges and sacrifices are to be faced in the harmonisation of customs policies of the member states in the TFTA on both a legal and technological level?
d) Is there hope in regional integration and what lessons may be drawn from the EU as an advanced and relatively successful REC in terms of developing a legal and technological framework for customs systems for the TFTA?

Through the harmonisation of national customs legislative frameworks policies and technological systems, member states will be in a position to effectively contribute to the lowering of costs of trade between governments and business and in turn attract investment to the region. This mini-thesis therefore essentially, by and large seeks to draw a number of lessons from the EU as a CU in mapping a way forward for the TFTA and drafting a road map towards the development of common regional customs policies and systems whilst recognising understandable region-specific, developmental and technological evolution differences which may exist between the TFTA and the EU.

1.4 SIGNIFICANCE OF RESEARCH

Costs of trade are well recognised to be wasteful expenditure in international trade which do not add real value to goods and result in artificially high valuation of products to the end user at the bottom of the supply chain. The reduction of trade costs associated with conducting business in the region which will follow as a result of the simplification, streamlining and creation of uniform customs procedures and the development of an automated and interoperable electronic customs system for the TFTA region, over the medium to long term, will immensely benefit TFTA member states.

The heads of member states within the three REC's agreed to the establishment of a TFTA which would combine the existing member states of the three existing REC's, at a tripartite summit held in 2008.[20] This was in concordance with the vision propounded by the African Union (AU) of 'an integrated, prosperous and peaceful Africa, driven by its own citizens and representing a dynamic force in the global arena'[21] which has been translated by the TFTA on a sub-regional level to become a vision which aims to "improve the economic and social welfare of the citizens of the TFTA region through promoting regional economic growth by creating a conducive environment for regional trade to take place."[22]

In turn the region as an economic block will begin to reap the benefits of a uniform customs regime and system which is well known and easily understood by international traders and simultaneously gear the region into a position to adequately handle the increase in trade volumes and ongoing technological advances in the world of international trade and customs. The proposal put forward by this mini-thesis to develop harmonised customs processes and develop a single electronic customs system for TFTA member states will streamline customs procedures at national borders and points of entry to increase regional economic competitiveness and as a result, significantly reducing the costs of trade for international traders.

This is an essential proposal which will promote the regional development of customs from a legal and technological perspective and better position regional customs both for the medium to long term growth of the region. The harmonisation of customs laws and customs electronic systems will further give rise to legal and procedural certainty to international traders seeking to conduct business in the region. It is to be reiterated that the development and subsequent implementation of a single customs electronic system for the region will not be an event but a long term process.

The process of simplification and harmonisation of customs legislation and policies for TFTA member states can be achieved and will enable the adoption of a single automated and interoperable electronic customs system for the TFTA. This mini-thesis will propose that member states of the TFTA work towards the gradual development of a simplified, common

---

[20] COMESA-EAC-SADC Tripartite - institutional framework available at *http://www.comesa-eac-TFTA-tripartite.org/home* (accessed 4 May 2013).

[21] COMESA-EAC-TFTA Tripartite - vision and strategy available at *http://www.comesa-eac-sadc-tripartite.org/about/vision_strategy* (accessed 4 May 2013).

[22] COMESA-EAC-TFTA Tripartite - vision and strategy available at *http://www.comesa-eac-sadc-tripartite.org/about/vision_strategy* (accessed 4 May 2013).

electronic customs system for the region. This will see the creation of a single interconnected regional electronic customs system which will eliminate national discrepancies in the collection and calculation of customs duties and tariffs and usher in the introduction of a single window[23] paperless environment in the administration of regional customs and trade aimed at building a solid communication and administrative network linking all customs offices within the region operating at national borders and points of entry.

1.5 RESEARCH METHODOLOGY

There exists a plethora of writings and information on the topic of customs and trade facilitation from various sources including official documents and reports by the World Trade Organisation (WTO), the United Nations Conference on Trade and Development (UNCTAD) and the World Customs Organisation (WCO). This mini-thesis will critically engage current academic debates and theories on the harmonisation of regional customs policies and customs systems and further proceed to suggest a regional solution for the TFTA by proposing a harmonised legal and technological framework for customs processes.

This proposal will be based on a deduction and comparative analysis of other writings and academic sources on customs and trade facilitation processes by undertaking a critical evaluation and analysis of the experiences and challenges faced by the EU as a CU in creating a modernised customs code and developing a single streamlined interconnected and interoperable automated customs system.

By critically evaluating the challenges of the TFTA in its collective drive towards harmonisation of national customs processes and customs systems, this mini-thesis proposes that the TFTA develop the single window system and adopt a single automated and interoperable electronic customs system similar to that of the EU as an effort to make inroads towards reducing wasteful costs of trade for international traders seeking to legitimately conduct business in the TFTA region.

[23]UNCTAD Trust Fund for trade facilitation negotiations: technical note 13 available at http://unctad.org/en/docs/TN13_DocumentSimplification.pdf (accessed 4 May 2013).

1.6 SCOPE OF RESEARCH

Due to the broad nature of the topic of trade facilitation and customs and the varied topics which may be analysed under this discipline, this paper will place its focus specifically on the development by the COMESA-EAC-SADC TFTA of a single set of customs legislation and technological procedures for the region in an effort to increase certainty, efficiency and minimise the costs of trade for international traders seeking to conduct business in the region as a whole. The mini-thesis will undertake a study of the EU as a CU and seek to understand how the EU has successfully developed and harmonised its legislative framework and customs policies in order to create a single efficient automated and interoperable customs system for its processes and administration.

In order for international trade to work to the best advantage of the TFTA member states, bold steps should be taken to enhance the simplification of customs processes at a regional level and reduce the costs of trade for international traders doing business in the region. In developing the ideas of a harmonised regional customs framework and a single automated and interoperable electronic customs system which will allow for the exchange of information between national customs offices within the TFTA, it must be borne in mind that a balance must be struck between the need to simplify and harmonise the customs laws and develop a single automated and interoperable electronic customs system for the TFTA and the indisputable fact that member states customs systems are currently not interconnected, and are at varying stages of ICT development.

1.7 OVERVIEW OF CHAPTERS

This first chapter is an introduction and overview of the topic and identifies the salient points which will be addressed by the mini-thesis as a whole in summary form. It shapes out the arguments propounded by the paper and is a discussion of the background behind the topic and explains the rationale of undertaking the proposed study and the research objectives of same while identifying the limitations of the research undertaken.

Chapter two is an examination of the single window experience. It performs a study to evaluate the single window experience and the benefits of implementing this system to the

TFTA area. This chapter further critically examines the single window experience of the EU as a CU is also examined in order to achieve a holistic view and appreciation of this customs processing system.

Chapter three is an analysis of current TFTA efforts to harmonise customs laws and policies. This chapter seeks to undertake a critical analysis of the current efforts by TFTA member states in creating and developing harmonised customs legislation and policies throughout the region. These efforts will be critically evaluated by examining the efforts made so far, successes achieved and implementational hurdles encountered in the process.

Chapter four takes a look at the Customs Union of the EU specifically with regards to its development and modernisation. At this stage the mini-thesis undertakes a critical journey of appreciating the EU customs union. It focuses on the development by the CU of the EU of a modernised customs code, the migration of EU member states from single and fragmented customs electronic systems to a single interoperable customs system. In addition a critical look is taken at the challenges in implementation and disadvantages of a single interoperable system for the various member states within the EU.

Chapter five discusses proposals for developing a legal and ICT framework for the TFTA regional single window together with prospective challenges ahead which may be encountered in the process of harmonising national customs laws and procedures. This chapter seeks to critically evaluate whether the TFTA member states may make inroads at regional level with respect to trade facilitation by developing a single automated electronic customs system for the region. This is in addition to a look at some of the challenges to be anticipated when implementing the harmonisation of the national customs laws of the members of the TFTA.

Chapter six puts forwards recommendations and also presents a final conclusion to the mini-thesis. This chapter concludes the mini-thesis by summarising the points discussed and rounds off by proposing recommendations to address the anticipated challenges in achieving harmonisation of the legal and technological aspects of customs in the TFTA.

CHAPTER 2: THE SINGLE WINDOW EXPERIENCE

2.1 INTRODUCTION

This chapter undertakes a study which seeks to critically evaluate the single window experience within customs processing and the corresponding benefits of implementing this system for the members of the Tripartite Free Trade Agreement (TFTA). Businesses engaged in cross border trade (import and export) are required on the whole, to prepare and submit large volumes of information and documents to various governmental authorities in order to fully comply with import, export and transit-related regulatory requirements on a regular basis. This information and documentation oftentimes has to be submitted through several different agencies, each having and prescribing their own customised requirements, systems, forms and processes.

These extensive onerous requirements, together with their associated compliance costs, can easily become a serious burden to both governments and the business community and pose a serious barrier to the development of international trade for the TFTA. One approach directed towards addressing the problem of import and export businesses dealing with multiple regulatory agencies is the development of a single window processing system for customs. This is a processing system whereby trade related information and supporting documentation need only be submitted once at a single entry point by a trader or business entity.

This simplified procedure can vastly enhance the availability and handling of information, expedite and simplify information flows between traders and government and can result in a greater harmonisation and sharing of relevant data across governmental systems, bringing meaningful economic gains to all parties involved in cross-border trade.[24] The use of the single window facility by the members of the TFTA can result in improved effectiveness of official controls and can reduce costs for both governments and traders due to more efficient use of resources.

The single window customs processing system is a globally recognised trade facilitation concept which 'allows traders to lodge information with a single body to fulfil all import or

---

[24] McLinden .G et al *Border Management Modernisation* (2011) 4.

export related regulatory requirements.'[25] The World Customs Organization (WCO) has in place, a set of guidelines on single window data harmonisation which are designed to assist in harmonising and standardising government international trade information and data requirements in order to develop and implement a single window environment.[26] It denotes the coordinated exchange of electronic information with a particular focus on legislation, procedures, and Information and Communications Technology (ICT). It has an emphasis on paperless trading for customs clearance, for licence and permit approvals by government agencies, and in some cases, for transport and logistics activities associated with cargo import, export, transit, trans-shipment, and border management.[27]

The guidelines are based upon best practices and provide details on policy and organisational matters necessary to achieve the aimed harmonisation. In addition, these guidelines also provide tools which governments can employ to facilitate the harmonisation process and details on harmonisation.[28]

The single-window customs processing system enables international traders to comply with customs regulations of a target market jurisdiction by allowing traders to submit all the relevant regulatory documents required for the processing of the through fare of goods across borders at a single location or regulatory entity. The regulatory documents would include customs declaration forms, import or export permits, certificates of origin and trading invoices among other documents which may be required for the clearance of goods.[29]

A single window customs processing system creates a variety of benefits for a country or a regional economic grouping as it reduces the overall time it would take to clear goods, lowers associated processing costs, reduces paperwork and significantly reduces the costs of trade for traders in their dealings with government authorities when obtaining the relevant customs

[25] Economic Commission for Europe: 'The Single Window Concept' available at *http://unpan1.un.org/intradoc/groups/public/documents/UNECE/UNPAN019892.pdf* (accessed 4 May 2013).

[26] World Customs Organisation data model, Single window data harmonisation available at *http://www.mincomes.it/semproitalia/tavolo_strategico/8_documenti/WCO/Documenti/WCO_Data%20Model_for_SW.pdf* (accessed 4 May 2013).

[27] McLinden .G et al *Border Management Modernisation* (2011) 125.

[28] SADC Draft guidelines for coordinated border management. Available at *http://www.trademarksa.org/sites/default/files/publications/Guidelines%20%7C%20Draft%20SADC%20guidelines%20for%20Coordinated%20Border%20Management%20%7C%20A%20Practical%20Guide%20on%20Best%20Practices%20and%20Tools%20for%20Implementation.pdf* (accessed 4 May 2013).

[29]Economic Commission for Europe: The Single Window Concept. Available at *http://unpan1.un.org/intradoc/groups/public/documents/UNECE/UNPAN019892.pdf* (accessed 4 May 2013).

clearances to transport goods across national or economic borders[30]. This is vastly different from the traditional pre-single window processing environment where traders are required to deal with multiple government agencies which may be located in different places before a trader can obtain the requisite clearance documents to complete the processing of their imports or exports.

The single window is therefore a practical application of trade facilitation concepts directed at the reduction of non-tariff trade barriers which can deliver rapid benefits to all members of the TFTA. In this regard, the single window system in the area of customs administration is one of the most integral tools for simplifying international trade procedures. In its electronic form it replaces the manual processing of customs documents by the computer assisted treatment of electronically transmitted information. The use of the single window system for the TFTA reduces the costs of trade on a regional level through the standardisation of forms and documents, data requirements, simplification and computerisation of customs clearance procedures to accelerate the clearance of goods.[31]

The single window system also has the potential to strengthen regional customs operational efficiency for control through the implementation of standard procedures and the provision of full audit trails and mechanisms in addition to providing member states of the TFTA with accurate and timely statistics on foreign trade and revenue. As a complement to regional integration reforms for the TFTA, the single window system is an essential component of customs modernisation which also encompasses the alignment of customs procedures and documents with international standards, conventions and other instruments.[32] It must be recognised as well that a single window system has the capacity to provide a wide variety of services and facilities depending on its design and coverage.[5]

The idea and attraction of a regional single window for the TFTA is also spurred on by the increasing impetus in regional and international circles for greater connectivity between

[30] National single window facilitates trade in the Philippines. *http://www.crownagents.com/national-single-window-facilitates-trade-in-the-philippines.aspx* (accessed 4 May 2013).

[31] UNCTAD Trust Fund for trade facilitation negotiations: technical note 13 available at *http://unctad.org/en/docs/TN13_DocumentSimplification.pdf* (accessed 4 May 2013).

[32] UNCTAD Trust Fund for trade facilitation negotiations: technical note 13 available at *http://unctad.org/en/docs/TN13_DocumentSimplification.pdf* (accessed 4 May 2013).

countries, regions and across continents. The regional model of a single window system contemplated in this mini-thesis foresees the supranational, nation-to-nation exchange of trade information between national single windows of the TFTA.

From a comparative perspective of other regional economic communities, the Association of South East Asian Nations (ASEAN) was one of the first REC's to conceptualise a regional single window project. In 2005, it concluded the agreement to establish and implement the ASEAN single window, and followed this through in 2006 with the establishment of a protocol for that single window.[33]The ASEAN single window is the first regional initiative which strives to enhance regional connectivity.[34] It is defined as

> "The secured environment where national single windows integrate and operate. The ASEAN single window constitutes a regional facility to enable a seamless, standardized and harmonized routing and communication of trade and customs-related information and data for customs clearance and release from and to national single windows. Trade and related customs data and information will stay within, and belong to respective Member States."[35]

It is also pertinent to take a look at the European Union (EU) and the efforts it has made in achieving significant milestones towards developing an effective single window system. In this regard, and from a European context, the EU has developed two major single window initiatives which are firstly, the single window initiative of the Directorate-General taxation and customs union which aims at a community-level single window, and secondly, the maritime single window of the Directorate-General for mobility and transport which aims to provide electronic exchange between the operators of maritime transporters within the EU.[36] In this context, the single widow is an attractive system because of its ability to connect national single windows, including the existing evolutionary forms of single windows such as

[33] Koh Tat Tsen. J *Single Windows and Supply Chains in the Next Decade, ten years of single window implementation: lessons learned for the future* Discussion paper Global Trade Facilitation Conference (2011) available at *http://www.unece.org/fileadmin/DAM/trade/Trade_Facilitation_Forum/BkgrdDocs/TenYearsSingleWindow.pdf* (accessed 4 May 2013). (Hereinafter referred to as Koh Tat Tsen. J (2011)).

[34] Koh Tat Tsen. J (2011) available at *http://www.unece.org/fileadmin/DAM/trade/Trade_Facilitation_Forum/BkgrdDocs/TenYearsSingleWindow.pdf* (accessed 4 May 2013).

[35] Extract from the agreement signed by the ASEAN Economic Ministers at the 11th ASEAN Summit, Kuala Lumpur December 2005.

[36] Koh Tat Tsen. J (2011) available at *http://www.unece.org/fileadmin/DAM/trade/Trade_Facilitation_Forum/BkgrdDocs/TenYearsSingleWindow.pdf* (accessed 4 May 2013).

customs specific single windows, in global networks that will facilitate cross-border trade and the sharing of information between member states of the TFTA over the long term.

By improving communications, information exchange and mutual assistance of and between the different border agencies of the TFTA, member state borders can be managed more effectively.[37] The resultant deeper cooperation between member states of the TFTA in the realm of customs may well be a powerful and effective tool to facilitate trade.[38] While the TFTA will initially be a Free Trade Area (FTA) there are plans to gradually evolve the grouping into a Customs Union (CU) thereby advancing the proposal and argument of developing a single window system for the TFTA in the area of customs cooperation. The planned evolution from an FTA through to a CU and finally progressing to becoming a common market will demand effective controls of the internal borders and, eventually, of the external borders of the common market.

A modern, automated customs administration can bring about substantial cost savings in trade and transport logistics. The electronic lodging of customs declarations, document processing and goods clearance brings substantial time savings and predictability to all aspects of cross-border trade and limits the room for manoeuvre by unscrupulous traders and customs officials alike to circumvent a system. The collection of taxes and duties is also enhanced, as is the statistical database for fiscal and economic policy purposes. In addition, as part of the process of the automation of customs, the working relationships between customs and the private sector improve.

More specifically, the benefits of automation include the faster electronic lodgement of customs declarations, the use of online connections, reduced customs clearance times and less physical examination of shipments owing to the use of risk management applications, increased collection of duties and taxes and less fraud due to the uniform application of laws

---

[37] SADC Draft guidelines for coordinated border management. Available at *http://www.trademarksa.org/sites/default/files/publications/Guidelines%20%7C%20Draft%20SADC%20guidelines%20for%20Coordinated%20Border%20Management%20%7C%20A%20Practical%20Guide%20on%20Best%20Practices%20and%20Tools%20for%20Implementation.pdf* (accessed 4 May 2013).

[38] SADC Draft guidelines for coordinated border management. Available at *http://www.trademarksa.org/sites/default/files/publications/Guidelines%20%7C%20Draft%20SADC%20guidelines%20for%20Coordinated%20Border%20Management%20%7C%20A%20Practical%20Guide%20on%20Best%20Practices%20and%20Tools%20for%20Implementation.pdf* (accessed 4 May 2013).

and regulations and the automated calculation of duties and taxes as well as built-in security.[39]

In practice, the single window processing system allows a trader to submit, either physically or electronically, all data and documentation related to the release and clearance of goods by one central agency which then has the function of informing other relevant agencies or alternatively, directing or coordinating combined control over the entire process.[40]

The creation and development of the TFTA regional single window for customs to facilitate the efficient flow of goods across national borders within the region will be an important factor in increasing the economic performance of the economic area. The TFTA covers a vast area in Africa and seeks to integrate three Regional Economic Communities (REC's). This is in itself a project of mammoth proportions but once implemented the issue of creating and developing a single window system for the region will be a pertinent issue to be addressed without delay if the TFTA is to bear any economic advantage for its member states.

The three REC's have to date identified infrastructure development and trade arrangements as starting points and priority areas for harmonisation into the TFTA. This proposed harmonisation being based on the premise that all the REC's will implement similar and corresponding customs programmes. In the area of customs, the three REC's have agreed that the desired focus will be on the harmonisation of among other things, customs laws, customs valuations, tariff nomenclatures and customs documentation.[41] Building on this, the three REC's have become conscious of the importance of a unified customs ICT system and as a result, agreed to develop a common customs network to allow for information exchange and transmission across the region.[42]

---

[39] UNCTAD Trust Fund for Trade Facilitation Negotiations Technical Note No. 3 Use of Customs automated systems available at *http://r0.unctad.org/ttl/technical-notes/TN03_CustomsAutomationSystems.pdf* (accessed 4 May 2013).

[40] Economic Commission for Europe: The Single Window Concept available at *http://unpan1.un.org/intradoc/groups/public/documents/UNECE/UNPAN019892.pdf* (accessed 4 May 2013).

[41] Disenyana, Tsidiso. SAIIA Discussion Paper, '*Towards an EAC, COMESA and SADC Free Trade Area: Issues and Challenges.*' available at *http://www.afdb.org/fileadmin/uploads/afdb/Documents/Knowledge/2009%20AEC-%20Towards%20an%20EAC%20COMESA%20and%20SADC%20Free%20Trade%20Area%20Issues%20and%20Challenges.pdf*. (accessed 4 May 2013).

[42] Disenyana, Tsidiso. SAIIA Discussion Paper, '*Towards an EAC, COMESA and SADC Free Trade Area: Issues and Challenges.*' available at *http://www.afdb.org/fileadmin/uploads/afdb/Documents/Knowledge/2009%20AEC-%20Towards%20an%20EAC%20COMESA%20and%20SADC%20Free%20Trade%20Area%20Issues%20and%20Challenges.pdf*. (accessed 4 May 2013).

An important distinction between FTA's and CU's is that the latter have, in addition to the internal free trade characteristic of FTA's, a common external tariff or, strictly, a common trade policy toward third countries. FTA's are less onerous to create and can be institutionally far less demanding, whereas CU's require the negotiation of a common external tariff and coordination of all future trade policy changes.[43]

FTA's unlike CU's however face the danger of trade deflection, where goods enter a member state with the lowest tariff and then move tax free to other member states. Governments seek to prevent this from happening by imposing rules of origin to ensure that only locally produced goods are exempted from tariffs. Such rules are often cumbersome and protectionist and can greatly reduce the value of the FTA. By developing into a CU, the TFTA could well avoid this problem and can propel a greater degree of integration.[44]

2.2 SELECTING A SUITABLE SINGLE WINDOW MODEL

There are three basic models for the single window[45] which the TFTA may consider in the implementation of this system for a regional response to customs modernisation and administration. These models are set out below as follows:

2.2.1 The single authority model.

In terms of this model, information which is submitted by a trader, either on paper or electronically, is disseminated from a central authority to all other relevant governmental authorities and the central authority co-ordinates controls to prevent undue hindrance in the logistical chain. For example, in the Swedish single window, customs performs selected tasks on behalf of some authorities, primarily for the National Tax Administration (import VAT),

---

[43] Schiff M and Winters A. L, *Regional integration and development* (2003) 16.

[44] Schiff M and Winters A. L, *Regional integration and development* (2003) 16.

[45] Ponten J, 'Single window – best practice and the way forward' Discussion paper *UNCITRAL colloquium on electronic commerce* New York, USA, February 14-16th 2011 available at http://www.uncitral.org/pdf/english/colloquia/EC/Ponten_SW_Best_Practice_and_the_Way_Forward.pdf (accessed 4 May 2013).

Statistics Sweden (trade statistics), the Swedish Board of Agriculture and the national Board of Trade (import licensing).[46]

2.2.2 Single automated system model for collection and dissemination of information.

This model integrates the electronic collection, use, dissemination and storage of data related to trade that crosses the border. For example, the United States has established a program which allows traders to submit standard data only once and the system processes and distributes the data to the agencies that have an interest in the transaction.[47]

2.2.3 The automated information transaction model

In terms of this model, a trader can submit electronic trade declarations to the various authorities for processing and approval in a single application. In this approach, approvals are transmitted electronically from governmental authorities to the trader's computer. Such a system is in use in Singapore and Mauritius.[48] When establishing this model, consideration could be given to the use of a central database, which consists of specific identities, which are pre-identified and pre-validated in advance for all relevant transactions.

The appropriate agency to lead the establishment and operation of a single window for the region will depend on political and organisational issues. The main agency must be a strong organisation with the necessary vision, legal authority, political backing, financial and human resources and interfaces to other key organisations. Due to its pivotal role, the information and documentation it receives and its key position at borders, customs or port authorities could be the agency best suited to lead a single window development and implementation programme.

---

[46] Koh Tat Tsen. J (2011) available at http://www.unece.org/fileadmin/DAM/trade/Trade_Facilitation_Forum/BkgrdDocs/TenYearsSingleWindow.pdf (accessed 4 May 2013).
[47] Koh Tat Tsen. J (2011) available at http://www.unece.org/fileadmin/DAM/trade/Trade_Facilitation_Forum/BkgrdDocs/TenYearsSingleWindow.pdf (accessed 4 May 2013).
[48] Koh Tat Tsen. J (2011) available at http://www.unece.org/fileadmin/DAM/trade/Trade_Facilitation_Forum/BkgrdDocs/TenYearsSingleWindow.pdf (accessed 4 May 2013).

In addition, customs could also be in charge of the central points to receive and coordinate the flow of information related to the fulfilment of all cross-border regulatory requirements. In all this however, the main organisation does not necessarily have to be a governmental organisation; it could alternatively also be a private entity such as a quasi-state organisation or a public-private-partnership. However, private organisations often lack the legal authority required to issue and accept information and documents and the power to enforce rules.

The ideal modern customs system must essentially be simple and transparent but at the same time should not be simplistic. This is because customs have to cope with a wide range of diverse issues many of which pose considerable danger to revenue and other policy objectives. The stage at which each national customs system is and the particular system in use will influence the appropriate single window model to adopt for the TFTA member states and the complementary reforms essential to undertake a unification of the various national customs systems into one regional customs system. For the single window model to be successfully implemented and further work effectively, the first step to be addressed by the TFTA member states is the simplification of information flows.

The theory of a single window model for customs further has broad implications for electronic government as it essentially involves government to government, government to business, and business to business exchanges. Once a single window system is implemented and adopted for the TFTA, information will be more readily available, improving handling, simplifying and expediting information flows between trade and government. Facilitating trade assists in deepening regional integration and trust through increased cooperation on border and customs policies which are highly sensitive areas.

Therefore the TFTA may actually promote cooperation and the development of shared information in a context broader than customs integration. It is noteworthy that similar to the creation of TFTA, the European Economic Community (EEC), the forerunner of the EU was created largely for political reasons and specifically regarded as an instrument to prevent conflict among European economies through increased trade and economic integration. It then evolved into a customs union, then further into a common market, and finally a monetary union.[49]

---

[49] McLinden G et al, *Border Management Modernization* (2011) 234.

2.3 MOTIVATION FOR A REGIONAL SINGLE WINDOW MODEL

According to McLinden[50] *et al*, increased cooperation on a regional level can be used to develop common responses to emerging challenges. By adopting a uniform and interconnected single window framework across the TFTA, members will be bound to stick to the common policies of the TFTA. This resultant policy lock-in enables member states to lock in and align domestic economic measures to regional economic reform measures in the medium to long term. An international legal commitment to a uniform single window system will therefore make it more onerous for a rogue member state to reverse painful but necessary long term commitments without incurring retaliation or a loss of confidence from other member states and private investors.

It is acknowledged that developing countries are turning increasingly to regionalism as a development tool;[51] however it remains that REC's vary from each other in terms of the extent to which they each approach the theory of policy integration.[52] Many REC's embody only the minimum requirements essential to implement a free trade agreement or a customs union, while others commit toward full integration of their domestic policies. More often than not, it also follows that the deeper the level of integration of a REC, the more likelihood there exists that the member states will reap tangible and meaningful benefits from the REC.

Effective regional integration demands more than the mere reduction of tariffs and quotas. It must be recognised that there also exist other forms of barriers which have the effect of segmenting markets and impeding the free flow of goods, services, investments, and ideas, and wide ranging policy measures, going well beyond traditional trade policies, such as fragmented domestic customs legislation and customs systems which are not interlinked.

A properly implemented regional customs ICT system linked to corresponding improvements in national customs practices will result in overall enhanced regional customs control over international consignments, improved control of exemptions, concessions and duty suspension regimes, reduced cargo clearance times for the discharge of customs formalities

---

[50] McLinden G et al, *Border Management Modernization* (2011) 235.
[51] Schiff M and Winters A. L, *Regional integration and development* (2003) 3.
[52] Schiff M and Winters A. L, *Regional integration and development* (2003) 174.

and closer cooperation and rationalisation of customs activities with other border control agencies in the TFTA region.

The proposed single window system should be implemented across the member countries in a coordinated and appropriate fashion taking into consideration regional and national needs whilst taking into account long term support, maintenance and flexibility. The common focus therefore should be on an upgrade; rationalisation and interlinking of the various national customs systems while aiming to attain a uniform level of technological sophistication where all information is exchanged electronically and decisions on treatment of consignments are made on a risk management basis.

In terms of this system, customs resources are optimised and shift to a low resource requirement where there is high value pre-arrival clearance and post-event systems based verification audit activity from a resource-intensive low value activity scenario at the time of arrival of a consignment. According to De Wulf and Sokol,[53] all customs administrations in developed economies are now working towards achieving this method of operation.

For implementation of the single window to be a success, a number of conditions however must be met from the onset. Firstly, the automation process must be transparent in order for it to gain positive momentum and support from all players involved who would include the governments of the TFTA members, and the private sectors of the various member states. Secondly, the automation must occur in phases with periodical reviews of targets and critical review of progress and system successes. This implementation should invariably occur at the same time during which the implementation of international conventions, standards and other instruments, including a regional customs tariff based on the harmonised system and documentation based on the United Nations layout key[54] takes place.

Finally, the automation should run concurrently with an overall review and amendment of customs laws and other related legal instruments by the member states of the TFTA to ensure compatibility with the new procedures, notably the electronic lodgement of clearance data and the introduction of a Single Administrative Document (SAD), where applicable.

---

[53] De Wulf .L and Sokol J.B *Customs Modernization Handbook* (2005) 288.

[54] UNCTAD Trust Fund for trade facilitation negotiations: technical note 13 available at http://unctad.org/en/docs/TN13_DocumentSimplification.pdf (accessed 4 May 2013).

2.4 DEVELOPING A BESPOKE SINGLE WINDOW MODEL FOR THE TFTA

Designing a regional customs system may be expensive and involve the commitment of huge financial outlay by the member states involved. Despite this, there is much to be gained from a careful scrutiny of the software products on the market and to review in a flexible and critical manner how to adapt same and develop a bespoke customs ICT system for the TFTA. Such a customs system should ideally be designed to allow the creation of an electronic network across the TFTA. It should ensure automated exchange of information among the various agencies involved through a unified system, including an intranet and internet system. Further, it must allow for a standardised system of collecting, processing and distributing data and information with real-time access for authorised users enabling data flow management at a centralised point which will facilitate links between the various agencies on board.[55]

The main functions of a customs administration are to control the cross-border flow of goods, to ensure compliance with government rules and regulations, collect the duties and taxes due according to the national customs tariff and tax codes (in the case of the TFTA, the regional tariff), and protect the region against the import of goods and materials intended for illegal purposes, and against terrorist activities. This complex work can be facilitated through the use of customs systems consisting of comprehensive and integrated software packages with a number of functionalities or modules.[56]

The single window customs system adopted should include such functionalities as cargo control which monitors all movements of import, transit and export, and ensures that all goods are either duly cleared before release or a mechanism is in place that allows for the release prior to clearance; declaration processing, for the capturing and processing of data for duty and tax collection; payment and accounting, to enable the registration of traders and account for payments by same; intelligence operations, to store and exchange data between national customs administrations within the TFTA for risk profiling and enforcement, and risk management to select consignments bearing a higher risk of concealing duties and taxes, or those prone to smuggling and trafficking illegal substances and materials; and lastly, statistic and reporting to enable the extraction of data for trade statistics.[57]

---

[55] Lakshmanan T et al, *Integration of Transport and Trade Facilitation Selected Regional Case Studies,* (2011) 33
[56] Lakshmanan T et al, *Integration of Transport and Trade Facilitation Selected Regional Case Studies,* (2011) 32
[57] Lakshmanan T et al, *Integration of Transport and Trade Facilitation Selected Regional Case Studies,* (2011) 33.

The single window is often associated with very sophisticated ICT systems. This is partly because the existing ICT systems which are marketed as possible examples are very sophisticated because they are systems which provide solutions for bringing a large number of international trade stakeholders together. The single window is essentially for an enabling economic operator to make one declaration which will serve the purposes of the various border agencies concerned. In its crudest form the single window can be implemented without ICT by placing all the agencies at one place which would be served by one document reception and vetting window.

The use of ICT will enhance facilitation but how sophisticated the ICT solution should be should depend on need and affordability.[58] It should in its element be able to complete three processes of single submission of documents by a trader onto the system, single processing by the customs administration and single release of the goods. To fulfil the above, a trader should be familiar with the process on a regional level and all the processes should be similar for all the countries in the TFTA.

This standardisation then enables a trader through the single window system, to complete requisite documents to satisfy all import, export and transit requirements on one platform and be able to reduce clearance times for goods. This then introduces the fact that the single window requires an ICT platform from which it can be run. In doing so, it becomes crucial to recognise that at present most of the customs administrations in the region make use of the United Nations Conference on Trade and Development (UNCTAD) customs ICT system known as the Automated Systems for Customs Data (ASYCUDA).

The ASYCUDA system has different versions and the member states of the TFTA could choose to migrate to the latest version of this system and ensure that their system is similar and interconnected in certain aspects for sharing of data between the different national customs administrations in the TFTA. Countries already using ASYCUDA could migrate to the latest version of ASCYCUDA which has been developed and adapted to have a single window portal and modules which link to customs and other government agencies. This

[58] SADC Draft guidelines for coordinated border management available at *http://www.trademarksa.org/sites/default/files/publications/Guidelines%20%7C%20Draft%20SADC%20guidelines%20for%20Coordinated%20Border%20Management%20%7C%20A%20Practical%20Guide%20on%20Best%20Practices%20and%20Tools%20for%20Implementation.pdf* (4 May 2013).

latest version is called ASYCUDA World and comes with an internet enabled front end which will enable national customs administrations to connect to the system.[59]

ASYCUDA was developed in modular form and this is where some of its greatest benefits derive from. The modularity of ASYCUDA means that new or advanced programmes (modules) can be added on at any time to suit the needs of a given country. The add-on modules could be expanded or developed to encompass customs functions such as risk management, transit operations or new security standards, depending on regional priorities.

Further to the above, the technical advantages of the ASYCUDA ICT customs system lie in the fact that it allows for multi language use and enables translation into various languages and also has user authentication security features which are built in to the system. Currently, ASYCUDA represents UNCTAD's largest technical cooperation and capacity-building programme worldwide and has been implemented in more than 90 countries. This system would therefore be advantageous rather than procuring very costly single window ICT systems especially as the ASYCUDA system is a proven and reliable system which has reliable maintenance by UNCTAD and has a very large user community.[60]

In addition to the above, the objectives of the ASYCUDA system are aligned to the objectives in this thesis of streamlining customs processes and creating a regional customs ICT system which encourages trade facilitation through the normalisation/standardisation of forms and documents and data standardisation. As a system it also aids in strengthening the operational efficiency and control of customs by providing modern tools and techniques for the implementation of sound procedures and the provision of full audit trails and mechanisms for controlling customs operations; and the streamlining and simplification of customs procedures and documentation; ASYCUDA also has the ability to be used to align national (and regional) trade documents with international standards for forms for example according to the United Nations layout key, the SAD, and documentation and data elements as contained in international conventions and recommendations, for example the World Customs Organisation (WCO) data model.

[59] General benefits of ASYCUDA World available at *http://www.asycuda.org/awbenefits.asp* (accessed 4 May 2013).

[60] General benefits of ASYCUDA World available at *http://www.asycuda.org/awbenefits.asp* (accessed 4 May 2013).

The Revised Kyoto Convention[61] provides standards and comprehensive guidelines for the application of ICT in customs and the TFTA could well benefit by applying the given guidelines when adopting a single window system for the region. Chapter seven of the Kyoto Convention states that information technology should be applied to support customs operations. This gives strength to the need to identify an electronic customs processing system which works well for the TFTA.

In addition, the ICT system which is eventually adopted, as a minimum, should comply with relevant internationally accepted standards.[62] When implementing a single window, governments and traders are strongly encouraged to consider the use of existing recommendations, standards and tools that have been developed over the past number of years by intergovernmental agencies and international organisations such as United Nations Economic Commission for Europe (UNECE), UNCTAD and the WCO. The use of recognised standards and available tools will help ensure that the systems developed to implement the single window are more likely to be compatible with similar developments in other countries, and could also help in the exchange of information between such facilities over time.

When the TFTA decides on a system and begins to develop that system, it is also highly advisable that the private sector is involved and allowed to participate before the roll out as they will also use the system at the front end. This idea is also supported by the Kyoto Convention which states that when introducing an ICT system, all the relevant parties who will be directly affected by the new system should be consulted to the greatest extent possible.[63]

A single window is a practical model for cooperation between government agencies, government to government and also between government and trade. It presents a good opportunity for a public-private-partnership in the establishment and operation of the system. Consequently, representatives from all relevant public and private sector agencies should be invited to participate in the development of the system from the outset. This should include

[61] International Convention on the Simplification and Harmonisation of Customs Procedures , Kyoto,1973.
[62] International Convention on the Simplification and Harmonisation of Customs Procedures , Kyoto,1973 chapter 7.2
[63] International Convention on the Simplification and Harmonisation of Customs Procedures , Kyoto,1973 chapter 7.3

participation in all stages of the project, from the initial development of project objectives, situational analysis, and project design through to implementation. The ultimate success of the single window will depend critically on the involvement, commitment and readiness of these parties, to ensure that the system becomes a regular feature of their business process.

2.5 CONCLUSION

The single window system is not the elixir to all of customs woes, but only a means that should lead to better customs operation. The computerisation of customs processes is likely to bring about the full advantage of process improvements if complemented by associated changes to legislation, a review of organisational structures, and enhanced operational procedures. The failure to incorporate these associated institutional reforms will deter the single window system from fully achieving its role as a catalyst for regional economic growth.[64]

In this vein, it follows that a carefully coordinated introduction and consolidation of the single window system even when unaccompanied by the latest customs modernisation features, can lead to the simplification and acceleration of clearance procedures, and the promotion of revenue mobilisation. To develop a single window is typically a massive undertaking involving interlinking and information sharing by customs and all government agencies responsible for trade, and also the trading community. It requires new ways of processing trade and necessitates streamlined business processes. Due to the complex change management involved, single window development typically follows a gradual evolutionary and staged pathway, usually starting from an advanced customs solution, and progressing to encompass advanced national and regional trade facilitation objectives.[65]

Particularly in developing countries and transition economies, the national single window has been a success story. Single window projects have simplified and automated business procedures, introduced change and brought about collaboration between government agencies and the private sector. Many countries which have implemented the single window system have shown marked improvements in their trade facilitation indicators, as seen in the various

[64] De Wulf L and Sokol J.B *Customs Modernization Handbook* (2005) 293.
[65] De Wulf L and Sokol J.B *Customs Modernization Handbook* (2005) 293.

surveys including the World Bank's *Doing Business - Trading across Borders*[66], as well as the Logistics Performance Index.[67]

In many advanced trading economies, such as the EU, the United States of America (USA) and China, the national single window concept has not been implemented in a generic form. This is due to the fact that these jurisdictions have instead implemented other forms of single window models, for example, port community systems and customs single windows which are limited forms of the single window and cover a specific procedure or a specific area. These limited forms of the single window can however still be successfully used to enhance a high volume logistics sector.[68] Linking these different platforms into a national or regional network however remains a challenge. Both in developed and developing countries, finding improved ways to conduct cross-border trade transactions is now an imperative and pressing need.

Trade liberalisation and regional integration are main drivers for a regional single window framework that facilitates cross-border trade exchanges. Many aspects of regional single window integration remain to be defined and these will be discussed in more detail in chapter three.[69] This includes data harmonisation, creating an effective legal framework for data exchange within a single window network, and a sustainable business model for the service providers. The future for global exchanges of information in inter regional supply chains is remote, as there is currently no framework for data exchange on a global level.

Over the last 10 years, single window projects have been mainly at the national level. For example, Zimbabwe adopted the ASYCUDA system in 1991 and has moved from the basic ASYCUDA model through to the latest model which ASYCUDA World is, becoming the first state within the Common Market for East and Southern Africa (COMESA) REC to

---

[66] Trading across borders, Doing business-the World Bank Group available at http://www.doingbusiness.org/data/exploretopics/trading-across-borders (accessed 4 May 2013).

[67] Logistic Performance Index, World Bank available at http://web.worldbank.org/WBSITE/EXTERNAL/TOPICS/EXTTRANSPORT/EXTTLF/0,,contentMDK:21514122~menuPK:3875957~pagePK:210058~piPK:210062~theSitePK:515434,00.html (accessed 4 May 2013).

[68] Koh Tat Tsen. J (2011) available at http://www.unece.org/fileadmin/DAM/trade/Trade_Facilitation_Forum/BkgrdDocs/TenYearsSingleWindow.pdf (accessed 4 May 2013).

[69] Koh Tat Tsen. J (2011) available at http://www.unece.org/fileadmin/DAM/trade/Trade_Facilitation_Forum/BkgrdDocs/TenYearsSingleWindow.pdf (accessed 4 May 2013).

migrate to ASYCUDA World. Despite these developments and improvements to its national project, it remains unconnected to any other national customs system in the REC. While these national efforts have been useful to governments for supporting the national economic agenda, they have increasingly become a major platform for an integrated world economy. This trend will increase the complexity and demands on single window projects. It is undeniable that there is a growing need for implementers of single windows to establish further international collaboration to develop common interconnectivity strategies, policies, data harmonisation and standards.

The Pan Asia E-Commerce Alliance (PAA) and their African counterpart, African Alliance for e-commerce (AACE) are examples of collaborating single window operators who have established a mechanism and framework for the conduct of secure cross-border document and data interchanges amongst the relevant stakeholders in their respective Asian and African regions. However, these efforts are only part of the picture and need to be complemented by the corresponding government policies to truly effect cross border exchanges.

Single window developments have come a long way from being just an idea to playing an integral and effective role in trade facilitation. What started as a concept has now become a clarion call for improving trade facilitation, transforming the economic development of many countries and economies. Taking into account the experiences from single window development, it is well worth suggesting that national governments in the TFTA and key stakeholders from the private sector community collaborate on key initiatives[70] to support and guide the future development of a regionally networked single window system. These initiatives should focus on the following aims:

a) To create a common, regional framework for single window planning and development that encompasses and interconnects different forms of single window models that are currently in use by the various member states in the TFTA. The use of a standard evolutionary model for single window development will greatly assist policymakers to

---

[70] Koh Tat Tsen. J (2011) available at http://www.unece.org/fileadmin/DAM/trade/Trade_Facilitation_Forum/BkgrdDocs/TenYearsSingleWindow.pdf (accessed 4 May 2013).

determine and ascertain the state of their national single window systems and define objectives for the next step of implementation.

b) Prioritising regional single window collaboration. Depending on the readiness of the member states of the TFTA, this could include the exchange of best practices, the development of sustainable business models and pilot projects for data exchange among national single windows, the development of technical and legal frameworks for information exchange and supporting trade agreements and policies.
c) Developing a vision at the regional level of how best to achieve electronic information exchange in regional supply chains using the capabilities of single window implementations in the member states of the TFTA. Such a vision must take into account the different single window models of the various affected countries and emerging technologies and requirements of international trade; and
d) Ensuring that policymakers take into consideration the potential of the regional single window system when developing bilateral or multilateral trade agreements. Those agreements should include provisions to enable information sharing in cross-border trade for use, security and efficiency.

After the above has been taken into consideration, it remains plain truth that the most important prerequisites for the successful implementation of a single window facility are the political will of the governments which will be involved in the regional single window project and the relevant governmental authorities concerned including the full support and participation of the business community. Further and fundamental to the success of the single window will also be the development of a standard legal framework, including the introduction of supranational and domestic privacy laws and regulations which would provide for the protection of privacy, preservation of integrity and security in the exchange of information, will also have to be developed by the member states of the TFTA.

CHAPTER 3: AN ANALYSIS OF TFTA EFFORTS TO HARMONISE CUSTOMS LAWS AND POLICIES

3.1 BACKGROUND

The decision to negotiate an agreement for the creation of a Tripartite Free Trade Agreement (TFTA) was sanctioned by heads of government for the Common Market for East and Southern Africa (COMESA), East Africa Community (EAC), and Southern African Development Community (SADC) Regional Economic Communities (REC's) at the first tripartite summit which was held in Kampala, Uganda in 2008.[71]

At the tripartite summit the importance of the envisaged tripartite agreement as a crucial stepping stone towards the eventual achievement of the African Economic Community (AEC) was emphasised as it is acknowledged that the TFTA is part of the pan-African vision towards one continental economic grouping.[72] This vision is a product of the Abuja treaty (1991) which was signed by several Organisation of African Union (OAU) heads of state and government. The Abuja treaty laid the groundwork for the creation of the AEC, with the REC's serving as building blocks for the envisaged continental community.

The TFTA is based on three main pillars which are identified as market integration, infrastructure development and industrial development. These three pillars further devolve to encompass other sub-areas which are in turn more specifically directed towards particular areas of negotiation. The area of customs harmonisation falls under the pillar of market integration.[73] The developments which have taken place to date or are currently underway or planned for under this pillar are then critically analysed in this chapter.

At the inaugural tripartite summit there also were established, tripartite sectoral ministerial committees on trade, finance, customs, economic matters and home/internal affairs and a further sectoral ministerial committee on legal affairs. Moreover, it was approved that these

---

[71] COMESA-EAC-SADC Tripartite background available at http://www.comesa-eac-sadc-tripartite.org/about/background (accessed 4 May 2013).

[72] In 1980, the OAU extraordinary summit adopted the Lagos plan of action where African leaders stated their commitment to work towards the eventual establishment of the African Economic Community.

[73] Hartzenberg T et al *The Tripartite Free Trade Area – Towards a new African Integration Paradigm?* (2012) 22. This is also contained in the Vision and Strategy document which was endorsed at the 2nd tripartite summit in June 2011.

ministerial committees would convene annually at the least and their implementing bodies which would assume the form of a tripartite taskforce of the secretariats of the three REC's would meet at least bi-annually.[74]

To date, the secretariats of the three REC's have successfully managed to complete a study aimed at the formation of a road map for establishing the TFTA, together with the legal and institutional framework to be developed for the region. A draft report and draft instruments were also circulated to the member states of the proposed TFTA.[75] The draft instruments which were developed consist of the TFTA agreement and its supporting annexures, tariff liberalisation modalities, rules of origin, the road map and the negotiating timetable.[76]

Of relevance to this theme will be the fact that the secretariats have held meetings on customs cooperation and as a result thereof, efforts to finalise a tripartite work programme in this area are at an advanced stage though they are not yet finalised.[77] These meetings include the 11th meeting of the subcommittee on customs and trade of the COMESA-EAC-SADC tripartite task force where it was reiterated that the three REC's should adopt harmonised standards and also work towards the development of a single regional framework for cooperation and mutual agreement.[78]

---

[74]SADC and the African Union - Tripartite Cooperation available at http://www.sadc.int/about-sadc/continental-interregional-integration/tripartite-cooperation/ (accessed 4 May 2013).

[75]Draft report and Instruments presented at the 2nd Tripartite Summit held on the 12 June 2011 in South Africa.

[76]SADC and the African Union - Tripartite Cooperation available at http://www.sadc.int/about-sadc/continental-interregional-integration/tripartite-cooperation/ (accessed 4 May 2013).).

[77]Report of the First Tripartite technical meeting on standards harmonisation held at Pretoria October 2010 available at http://www.trademarksa.org/sites/default/files/publications/REPORT%20OF%201ST%20TRIPARTITE%20TECH%20MEETING%20ON%20STANDARDS%20HARMONIZATION(final).pdf (accessed 4 May 2013) ; The Comprehensive Trade and Transport Facilitation Programme (CTTTFP) launched in 2011 is a series of initiatives from different RECs that have been brought together into one large integrated trade facilitation programme which includes: the NTB monitoring, reporting and removal system, border and customs procedures (one-stop border posts; integrated border Management, regional customs bond, transit management), immigration procedures, transport procedures (regional 3rd party insurance, vehicle standards and regulation, self-regulation of transporters, overload control, harmonised road user charges, regional corridor management systems and the establishment of the Joint Competition Authority linked to air transport liberalisation.

[78]Shayanowako P, 'Towards a Tripartite Free Trade Area' *Trade and development studies* Issue No. 40 (2011) available at http://www.panafricanglobaltradeconference.com/upload/towards_a_tripartite_free_trade_area_.pdf (accessed 4 May 2013).

The draft TFTA agreement contains an annexure[79] which specifically addresses the subject of the simplification and harmonisation of trade documentation and procedures in customs. This annexure to Article 14 of the draft TFTA agreement seeks to address this matter and states its objective as that of promoting cooperation among member states within the TFTA to simplify and harmonise trade documentation and procedures in order to facilitate intra-tripartite trade.

This annexure is a clear translation of the theory that the harmonisation of customs legislation, policies and data is the key towards developing successful customs modernisation initiatives and is the solution to unlocking and accelerating regional economic growth for the TFTA.[80] It is also of importance to take note of the fact that, since the inception of the TFTA, the three REC's have executed lone and fragmented attempts towards the coordination and harmonisation of their members' trade rules including the simplification of customs procedures and documentation, citing for example, the standardisation of the COMESA and SADC customs bond guarantee schemes.[81]

In addition the three REC's have, in their individual capacities also focused on the advancement of customs training and capacity building schemes, coordination of institutional frameworks, and the establishment of One Stop Border Posts (OSBP). A particular success story in the implementation of an OSBP is that of the Chirundu OSBP which is shared by Zimbabwe and Zambia.[82] The implementation of the OSBP concept at Chirundu has reaped a number of positive benefits to the trading community as well as the governments involved.

These benefits include a significant reduction in the prevalence and occurrence of fraudulent activities and rapid clearance of goods as trucks only stop once for all formalities resulting in

---

[79] Annexure 3 to the Draft Agreement Establishing the COMESA-EAC-SADC Tripartite Free Trade Area 2010.

[80] Dobronogov. A & Farole T 'An Economic Integration Zone for the East African Community Exploiting Regional Potential and Addressing Commitment Challenges' *Policy Research Working Paper* No. 5967 World Bank Africa Region Poverty Reduction and Economic Management Unit (2012) 5 available at http://www-wds.worldbank.org/external/default/WDSContentServer/WDSP/IB/2012/02/13/000158349_20120213133305/Rendered/INDEX/WPS5967.txt (accessed 20 April 2013).

[81] Otieno L. and Shinyekwa I 'Prospects and challenges in the formation of the COMESA-EAC-SADC Tripartite Free Trade Area' *Research Series 87 Economic Policy Research Centre* Nov. 2011 available at http://www.eprc.or.ug/pdf_files/series87.pdf (accessed 4 May 2013).

[82] Trade facilitation case study on customs cooperation between Zambia and Zimbabwe. Presented at the World Trade Organisation Symposium November 2011 Geneva available at https://www.wto.org/english/tratop_e/tradfa_e/case_studies_e/bac_zmb_e.doc (accessed 4 May 2013).

the reduction of the cost of trade.[83] While in the past vehicle clearance time took an average of four days from arrival to departure at Chirundu border, clearance time has been reduced down to twenty four hours on the proviso that all documents will be in order and the client is able to pay the requisite taxes immediately the assessment is issued. With the implementation of the OSBP at Chirundu, there has also been a related increase in intra-regional competitiveness attributable to the reduced costs of clearing of goods at the border.[84]

It is acknowledged that the TFTA is an ambitious proposal and therefore, it was agreed at the tripartite summit that it would be negotiated in two phases.[85] The first phase is of relevance to this chapter. The first phase of the negotiation process specifically focused on addressing matters which include the harmonisation of rules and regulations on goods, rules of origin, dispute resolution, customs procedures and the simplification of customs documentation and transit procedures. This negotiating stratagem inexorably raises a number of multifaceted issues as each identified issue is without doubt interlinked or connected to other issues identified in the phase.

The objective of the tripartite is to deal with the heterogeneity existent within national policy objectives, the alignment of standards and conformity assessment procedures, trade facilitation, the state of regional bloc progress and compliance to multilateral rules amongst others. Any failure therefore by the tripartite to generate substantive progress towards the attainment of the phase one issues may well endanger the transition to negotiating a successful agreement encompassing the phase two issues.[86]

Customs was identified in the phase one issues and its value and relevance to the success of the TFTA cannot be overemphasised. Thus far, the three secretariats of the REC's have been

---

[83] Kieck E, 'Coordinated Border Management: Unlocking trade opportunities through One Stop Border Posts' (2010) 4 *WCJ* 7 available at http://worldcustomsjournal.org/media/wcj/-2010/1/Kieck.pdf (accessed 4 May 2013).

[84] Trade facilitation case study on customs cooperation between Zambia and Zimbabwe. Presented at the World Trade Organisation Symposium November 2011 Geneva available at https://www.wto.org/english/tratop_e/tradfa_e/case_studies_e/bac_zmb_e.doc (accessed 4 May 2013).

[85] Tripartite FTA Negotiation Principles, Processes and Institutional Framework – Guidelines for negotiating the Tripartite Free Trade Area among the member/partner states of COMESA, EAC and SADC, 12 June 2011 available at http://www.trademarksa.org/sites/default/files/publications/Negotiating%20Principles%20%20-%2012.06.2011%20-%20English.pdf (accessed 4 May 2013).

[86] Otieno L. and Shinyekwa I 'Prospects and challenges in the formation of the COMESA-EAC-SADC Tripartite Free Trade Area' *Research Series 87 Economic Policy Research Centre* Nov. 2011 available at http://www.eprc.or.ug/pdf_files/series87.pdf (accessed 4 May 2013).

cooperating in an untailored framework through the tripartite task force, in the harmonisation and rationalisation of programs and instruments in respect of a number of essential areas of cooperation earmarked as programs of harmonisation of trade regimes of the three REC's and in the united implementation of regional projects and legal and institutional activities for regional cooperation.[87]

3.2 TRIPARTITE DEVELOPMENTS IN CUSTOMS POLICY AND LEGISLATIVE HARMONISATION

To date, substantial support has been extended to the tripartite in support of various customs reform and modernisation programs by the World Bank and United States Agency for International Development (USAID) at the national and regional level.[88] In this regard, the Comprehensive Tripartite Trade and Transport Facilitation Programme (CTTTFP) is the over-arching project through which a number of other tripartite projects are being administered.

In terms of the CTTTFP, regulatory and policy reforms which promote the harmonisation and adoption of international instruments and best practices in the area of customs by member states have been developed. These regulatory and policy reforms take account of efforts at national and regional level which are targeted at facilitating cross-border movements.[89] The CTTTFP has also sought to address assorted issues through its projects including customs legislation and procedures, the efficient management of border posts, the development of a single administrative customs document, cooperation on customs enforcement and the design and implementation of a harmonised regional customs bond.

The CTTTFP as an umbrella programme involves a number of diverse initiatives from the three REC's which have been brought together and are now administered under one over-

---

[87]Pearson M, 'Trade Facilitation in the COMESA-EAC-SADC Tripartite Free Trade Area' September 2011 available at *http://www.trademarksa.org/publications/trade-facilitation-comesa-eac-sadc-tripartite-free-trade-area* (accessed 4 May 2013).

[88] Chaitezvi C *Trade Facilitation in Eastern and Southern Africa: WTO Trade Facilitation Symposium, Geneva 2012* available at *https://www.wto.org/english/tratop_e/tradfa_e/case_studies_e/session6_trademark_e.ppt*. (accessed 4 May 2013).

[89] Pearson M, 'Trade Facilitation in the COMESA-EAC-SADC Tripartite Free Trade Area' September 2011 available at *http://www.trademarksa.org/publications/trade-facilitation-comesa-eac-sadc-tripartite-free-trade-area* (accessed 4 May 2013).

arching integrated trade facilitation programme. This programme encompasses initiatives in the areas of border and customs procedures as well as OSBP projects, integrated border management and regional customs bonds. The objectives to be addressed through the CTTTFP are aimed towards;

a) increasing trade and promoting economic growth in Eastern and Southern Africa through supporting developments in regional policies and in the regional regulatory and economic environment;
b) reducing the high costs of trade associated with conducting business in the region and to assist national administrations, working through the REC's, to address barriers to economic growth; and
c) dropping the transit times and transaction costs along the principal corridors in Eastern and Southern Africa through faster border crossings and harmonised trade and transit regulations.[90]

The CTTTFP has achieved considerable progress in a number of areas and programmes which include customs information communications technology (ICT) policies, integrated border management and regulatory reforms.[91] These developmental strides are critically discussed in more detail below.

3.2.1 Customs Information Communications Technology Policy and Connectivity

The importance of having an effective and efficient ICT processing system in customs cannot be overstated. It is vital for the successful operation of a whole host of modern customs operations including customs automation, cargo tracking, pre-arrival clearances, risk analysis, the electronic submission of documents; information management and electronic single windows.[92] Not only does an efficient ICT system enable faster processing times but it also increases revenue collection, reduces red tape and increases capacity and efficiency through

---

[90] The COMESA-EAC-SADC Tripartite trade and transport facilitation programme available at http://www.oecd.org/aidfortrade/47407250.pdf (accessed 4 May 2013).
[91] Regional Work Programme to harmonise and simplify customs procedures and legislation- TradeMark Southern Africa (TMSA) Advancing regional integration in Southern and Eastern Africa available at http://www.trademarksa.org/about_us/programme_news/regional-work-programme-harmonise-and-simplify-customs-procedures-and-legisl (accessed 4 May 2013).
[92] De Wulf L and Sokol J, B *Customs Modernization Handbook* (2005) 287-289.

the introduction of new and innovative systems which would otherwise be impractical to introduce in the absence of an efficient ICT system.

In the realm of ICT, the tripartite approved the provision of much needed support for transit trade facilitation and develop a joint programme for the implementation of an accelerated, seamless inter-regional ICT broadband infrastructure network including a harmonised policy and regulatory framework which will govern ICT development in the three REC's.[93]

Further to this, at a REC level, in the Southern African Development Community (SADC) REC, the first live display of an end to end customs connectivity solution was effectively conducted in Windhoek, Namibia on the 12th of December 2012.[94] Customs connectivity facilitates the sharing of information across borders and between customs administrations from various countries in a seamless manner. This decreases processing times and increases access to reliable real time statistics.

The demonstration involved the movement of information from an Automated Systems for Customs Data (ASYCUDA) World entry in Botswana through a cloud-based user portal to an ASYCUDA World entry in Namibia.[95] This was also effectively, a demonstration of how traders would administer the flow of their information through a safe regional online user portal. This innovative form of regional customs connectivity illustrates the potential of engaging revolutionary technology and modern tools to facilitate trade across the TFTA region as a whole.

The pilot project put into operation by Botswana and Namibia could well be extended across the entire TFTA region once it proves successful. This project is a successful example of work in progress towards regional integration in the area of customs.[96] It is envisaged that the

[93] Chaitezvi C *Trade Facilitation in Eastern and Southern Africa: WTO Trade Facilitation Symposium, Geneva 2012* available at https://www.wto.org/english/tratop_e/tradfa_e/case_studies_e/session6_trademark_e.ppt. (accessed 4 May 2013).

[94] Southern African Trade Hub – Regional Customs Connectivity Customs pilot programme available at http://www.satradehub.org/customs-connectivity/sath-content/activities/trade-facilitation/customs-connectivity (accessed 4 May 2013).

[95] Aid for Trade Global Review: Microsoft and the Trans-Kalahari Corridor Regional Single Window available at http://www.oecd.org/aidfortrade/48367286.pdf (accessed 4 May 2013).

[96]This pilot project is supported by USAID/SATH. During July 2011, SATH unveiled a plan to initiate a pilot project to link the ASYCUDA systems of Namibia and Botswana via Microsoft "cloud computing" technology.

system, which works through cloud computing will be able to maintain enormous volumes of transit data which will assist in future planning.

At the moment however, the model is still under improvement as there remain fragmentary technical issues to be addressed including matters of ownership rights to access, and integrity of use of information.[97]In addition it yet to be thoroughly understood how the system will be able to address issues relating to the integration of customs information, as there is considered to be a shortfall in the designing process in the sense that the end users in the form of the business community were not fully involved in the scope, proof of concept or design of the system.[98]

To date no automated system has been able to share customs information between countries in the three REC's making up the TFTA.[99] In customs operations, large quantities of the same information are required to prepare export documentation in one country and import documentation in another country for cross-border shipments, and due to lack of shared or connected customs processing systems across the region, all information and processes must be duplicated, effectively increasing the costs of trade and making African goods uncompetitive. This negative predicament could otherwise be avoided if the customs systems were interconnected.

Customs connectivity reduces repetitive data entry, opportunities for errors and fraudulent declarations, and in due course reduces the costs of exports and imports.[100] It ameliorates the compilation of standardised trade statistics for customs administrations and allows greater visibility of the cross-border trade process. It can also facilitate planning and risk assessment before goods arrive at the border and increase revenues through reducing duty avoidance. The connectivity pilot project has been designed in a manner where it will have minimal

[97] New Customs system launched. TradeMark South Africa TMSA) Advancing regional integration in Southern and Eastern Africa available at *http://www.trademarksa.org/news/new-customs-system-launched* (accessed 4 May 2013).

[98]Southern African Trade Hub – Regional Customs Connectivity Customs pilot programme available at *http://www.satradehub.org/customs-connectivity/sath-content/activities/trade-facilitation/customs-connectivity* (accessed 4 May 2013).

[99]NRA/BURS – Customs connectivity passes test: What happened to the Portcullis? Available at http://mpoverello.com/2013/01/24/namburs-customs-connectivity-passes-test/ (accessed 4 May 2013).

[100]Apostolov M, 'The Single Window and data harmonization in line with international standards' 7th Meeting of the CAREC Customs Cooperation Committee Issy-Kul, 8-9 Sept.2008 available at http://www.carecprogram.org/uploads/events/2008/7th-CCC/UNECE-Single-Window-Data-Harmonization.pdf (accessed 4 May 2013).

impact on current customs operations and minimal implementation costs for end users as traders can make use of an online portal to transfer export declaration data across borders and retrieve import declaration data through the existing ASYCUDA world user interface. In turn, customs officials are able to access trade and performance statistics through an online console.[101]

The cloud connectivity approach taken by the Botswana United Revenue Service and Namibian Customs eradicates the encumbrance of maintaining hardware or a regional data centre for the cloud-hosted processes. Cloud-based connectivity can also be further upgraded to provide more ICT resources swiftly as demand increases or as other service functions are developed. Disaster recovery is also efficiently and automatically handled by the cloud platform, improving the continuity of operations.[102]

3.2.1.1 Electronic Single Window

Electronic single windows decrease instances of duplication, increase speed, and can lower the costs of cross-border trade. In their absence, traders are required to put in order and submit the same information to multiple regulatory agencies before obtaining requisite clearances for goods to enter or leave a country. [103] Without the single window, regulatory agencies have to make clearance decisions individually based on the specific information they require, instead of conducting an overall assessment of the risk of any particular shipment compounding to the cost and time taken to cross borders.

The Southern Africa Trade Hub[104] is currently advocating the implementation of single windows in Malawi, Zambia, Botswana, South Africa, Namibia and Swaziland. This programme is being carried out in a variety of ways, namely through increasing public and private sector consciousness and appreciation of the single window as a trade facilitation tool,

[101] UNCTAD Trust Fund for Trade Facilitation negotiations Technical Note No. 21 ASYCUDA available at http://unctad.org/en/docs/TN21_Asycuda.pdf (accessed 4 May 2013).

[102] Southern African Trade Hub – Regional Customs Connectivity Customs pilot programme available at http://www.satradehub.org/customs-connectivity/sath-content/activities/trade-facilitation/customs-connectivity (accessed 4 May 2013).

[103] WCO Data Model Connects trade stakeholders available at http://www.wcoomd.org/en/topics/facilitation/resources/~/media/3267E6020CA044359C1B479F6515A93F.ashx (accessed 4 May 2013).

[104] Southern African Trade Hub – National Single Window available at http://www.satradehub.org/national-single-window/sath-content/activities/trade-facilitation/national-single-window (accessed 4 May 2013).

through supporting studies to define and determine necessary regulatory changes, assisting in the inclusion of a regional perspective throughout the designing phase of the national single windows in order to facilitate future linkages with neighbouring single windows and also through the provision of targeted assistance during implementation.[105]

Due to this programme by the Southern African Trade Hub, there has been noteworthy progress towards the establishment of single windows in Botswana, Namibia, Malawi, Zambia and Swaziland. In addition, the programme is also focused on rationalising cross-border regulatory documentation submission required of traders, reducing time and costs associated with the preparation of trade related documentation, reduce processing and clearance times and improving risk management by regulatory agencies.[106]

3.2.2 Integrated Border Management

Improved border efficiencies result in a mutually favourable situation for stakeholders. As a result thereof, governments gain revenue as there is an increase in the volume of goods crossing borders along with a higher level of control. Businesses gain as they receive inputs more rapidly and at more favourable landed costs. They are then in turn, able to deliver goods to customers at competitive prices who do not have to pay the hidden costs of lengthy border delays.[107]

The function of customs cooperation in the successful implementation of the TFTA is therefore crucial as it is the efficient performance of the TFTA arrangement which will enable the delivery of the intended benefits to the TFTA members. It is in this respect that customs plays an important role in ensuring the expeditious and smooth cross-border movement of goods in the TFTA. Customs cooperation is important due to the fact that customs authorities are the ones responsible for the cross-border clearance of goods traded.

---

[105]New Customs system launched. TradeMark South Africa TMSA) Advancing regional integration in Southern and Eastern Africa available at *http://www.trademarksa.org/news/new-customs-system-launched* (accessed 4 May 2013).

[106]Swaziland, trading across borders-TradeMark Southern Africa available at *http://www.trademarksa.org/news/swaziland-trading-across-borders* (accessed 4 May 2013).

[107]Engman M, O. Onodera and E. Pinali, 'Export Processing Zones: Past and Future Role in Trade and Development', *OECD Trade Policy Working Papers* (2007) No. 53 available at http://dx.doi.org/10.1787/035168776831 (accessed 4 May 2013).

As a consequence, issues related to border enforcement also rest squarely on customs. A number of countries in the proposed TFTA have accepted the OSBP concept and now aim to change most of their border posts to OSBP's.[108] In terms of this unique type of border post set up goods and passenger vehicles stop once at the border and exit from one country and enter another country at the same time. This has the effect of generating reductions in time and costs in border crossings.[109]

The main benefits of an OSBP are derived from the fact that border and customs authorities from two countries perform joint controls with resulting mutual benefits such as more efficient resource utilisation through a reduction in the duplication of processes. Each national customs authority handles traffic going in only one direction on either side of the border effectively improving enforcement efficiencies through co-operation and sharing of intelligence, improved communication and sharing of ideas, and experiences. [110]

According to Pearson[111], There are four core elements involved in the implementation of an OSBP;

a) legal framework, prepared nationally though the East Africa Community (EAC) is exclusively developing a regional framework;
b) design of procedures and traffic flows for the common control zone;
c) ICT; and
d) the design of physical facilities as a common integrated facility by the two countries involved.

As previously cited above, the Chirundu OSBP is a worthy illustration of how integrated border management can be harnessed as a force or means of generating economic efficiencies

---

[108]Pearson M, 'Trade Facilitation in the COMESA-EAC-SADC Tripartite Free Trade Area' September 2011 available at *http://www.trademarksa.org/publications/trade-facilitation-comesa-eac-sadc-tripartite-free-trade-area* (accessed 4 May 2013).

[109] Chaitezvi C *Trade Facilitation in Eastern and Southern Africa: WTO Trade Facilitation Symposium, Geneva 2012* available at https://www.wto.org/english/tratop_e/tradfa_e/case_studies_e/session6_trademark_e.ppt. (accessed 4 May 2013).

[110]Report of the Tripartite (COMESA, EAC and SADC) OSBP Workshop 26-27 October 2011 Johannesburg, South Africa available at *http://tis.sadc.int/files/4813/3068/3347/Report_-_Regional_OSBP_Workshop_2627_Oct_11_Johannesburg.pdf* (accessed 4 May 2013).

[111]Pearson M, 'Trade Facilitation in the COMESA-EAC-SADC Tripartite Free Trade Area' September 2011 available at *http://www.trademarksa.org/publications/trade-facilitation-comesa-eac-sadc-tripartite-free-trade-area* (accessed 4 May 2013).

through the reduction of border clearance times. Inasmuch as it is a busy border post handling daily average volumes of up to 400 trucks, it effectively manages to handle large volumes of goods, traffic and people. The border post is managed by the COMESA secretariat on behalf of the TFTA and is the first functioning one stop border post across the whole of Africa.[112]

The clearance times for passengers on 76-seater buses have also decreased from an average time of six hours down to less than two hours. Due to the fact that clearance times are reduced, more cargo carriers prefer Chirundu as their point of entry into, and point of exit out of, Zambia. Despite this increase in traffic volumes the border agencies are still able to clear all trucks arriving at the border in the same day.[113]

Undoubtedly, the integrated border management system is advantageous and valid at a national level, the challenge remains however, for the TFTA to transform this system and implement same on a regional scale. If the TFTA is to deliver optimal benefits in terms of realising progressively increasing levels of economic growth then the delivery of efficient customs administrative processes becomes more critical in the pursuit of regional economic success.

The challenge then posed for the tripartite is that of developing the regional single window concept and obtaining much needed cooperation from the various border agencies in the TFTA member states where the multi-national single window system will be launched an operated in. To carry through a successful programme in integrated border management, it is imperative that there is regulatory reform carried out as well which will address the disparities in domestic legislation and policy across the region.

3.2.3 Regulatory reform

Regulatory reform encourages the construction of bespoke regional agreements, legal frameworks, and trade facilitation instruments which often involves the harmonisation of

---

[112]Aid for trade case story: Zimbabwe-Chirundu One Stop Border Post, A Regional Trade Facilitation Programme available at http://www.oecd.org/aidfortrade/47750237.pdf (accessed 4 May 2013).
[113]Rippel B 'Why Trade Facilitation is Important for Africa' *Africa Trade Policy Notes, 27*, World Bank (2011) available at *http://siteresources.worldbank.org/INTAFRREGTOPTRADE/Resources/trade_facilitation_note_nov11.pdf* (accessed 4 May 2013).

trade related standards complementary to the conclusion of mutual recognition agreements. Since regional cooperation demands some form of official framework to support and implement integration and spur it forward there also exists an institutional element to this area. One of the common integration priorities for the TFTA is that of trade facilitation at borders to lower transaction costs to improve competitiveness and improve the coordination of trade facilitation activities. The customs harmonisation programmes under the CTTTFP are already working on the aspects identified earlier and are now discussed below;

3.2.3.1 Customs Tariff Nomenclatures and Statistical Nomenclatures

The World Customs Organisation (WCO) has developed a harmonised system for the categorisation of goods. This system makes use of a six-digit coding system. Most countries then further sub-categorise goods in more detail for statistical purposes and the purposes of applying other trade policy measures. The tripartite is currently aiming towards and working on harmonising the classification of the system of the classification of goods across the TFTA to the 7th and 8th digit level.[114]

3.2.3.2 The design and implementation of a harmonised regional customs bond

At the REC level, SADC and COMESA designed and piloted regional customs bond guarantee systems which allow traders to take out a single bond which covers an entire trip without having to take out various national customs bonds.[115] The challenge however is that of designing an approach which will provide insight on how to extract the best features of each of these two systems in order to merge them into one integrated system to the greater advantage of the TFTA. While a study on how this can be undertaken has been conducted, the practical harmonisation and implementation of such a single system is yet to take place.

---

[114] Aid For Trade Case Story - The COMESA-EAC-SADC Tripartite Trade and Transport Facilitation Programme available at http://www.oecd.org/aidfortrade/47407250.pdf (accessed 4 May 2013).

[115] COMESA-EAC-SADC Tripartite – Trade and transport facilitation: Focal Area 2 available at http://www.comesa-eac-sadc-tripartite.org/intervention/focal_areas/trade_facilitation (accessed 4 May 2013).

3.3 CUSTOMS AND LEGISLATIVE PROCEDURES

The three REC's have acknowledged in their respective treaties and protocols that the harmonisation of customs procedures is essential for the smooth operation of FTA's and the facilitation of intra-regional trade. As a result, the heads of customs across the REC's agreed that all member states would take the necessary measures to accede to and fully implement the Revised Kyoto Convention[116] (RKC) and that the REC's should provide the necessary technical assistance required for the implementation of the RKC.[117]

In this regard, a Department For International Development (DFID) funded, COMESA administered unit[118] was mandated with the task of assessing the progress made in implementation of RKC provisions by member states that have acceded to the convention and also to facilitate regional and national workshops on RKC to acclimatise and sensitise members on technical and financial support available at national level for accession to the convention.

All the tripartite member states endorse the aims and objectives of the RKC which aims to provide customs administrations with a modern set of uniform principles for simple, effective and predictable customs procedures which simultaneously enable the achievement of effective customs control. The RKC, in conjunction with the Istanbul Convention[119] which governs the temporary admission of goods, the Arusha Declaration,[120] which is a non-binding instrument that provides the basic principles to promote integrity and combat corruption within customs administrations and the Nairobi[121] and Johannesburg[122] Conventions which enable customs administrations to afford each other mutual assistance on a reciprocal basis,

---

[116]The International Convention on the Simplification and Harmonisation of Customs procedures, 1974.

[117]COMESA-EAC-SADC Tripartite – Trade and transport facilitation: Focal Area 2 available at *http://www.comesa-eac-sadc-tripartite.org/intervention/focal_areas/trade_facilitation* (accessed 4 May 2013).

[118]TradeMark Southern Africa is a £100 million, 5-year programme hosted by COMESA and funded by the UK's Department for International Development. This programme supports the work of the tripartite and has three main components which are; infrastructure development, trade policy capacity development and trade facilitation.

[119]The Convention Relating to Temporary Admission, 1990 (Istanbul Convention).

[120]The Arusha Declaration on Customs integrity, 1993.

[121]The International Convention on Mutual Administrative Assistance for the Prevention, Investigation and Repression of Customs Offences, 1977.

[122] The Revised International Convention on Mutual Administrative Assistance for the Prevention, Investigation and Repression of Customs Offences, 2003.

with a view to preventing, investigating, and repressing customs offences, address the requirements of customs administrations.

The texts of these conventions incorporate modern approaches towards providing a balance between the customs functions of control and revenue collection with that of trade facilitation and also warrant that customs carry out their duties more effectively, facilitating the international movement of goods whilst simultaneously ensuring compliance with national laws. A programme is therefore underway, under the CTTTFP flag to harmonise the activities currently being undertaken by the three REC's to simplify and harmonise customs procedures based on international best practices.[123] In terms of the CTTTFP programme the task force has a number of areas which are targeted for harmonisation and are elaborated upon below.

3.3.1 Trade Facilitation

In terms of this target or focal area, the tripartite task force has mandated work on the development of a harmonised single administrative customs document for the three REC's. The three REC's are also working on the standardisation of customs cooperation provisions for the exchange of information on changes in customs legislation, procedures and duties and information on regulatory requirements and information required to implement and administer rules of origin.[124]

3.3.2 Preservation, Investigation and Suppression of Customs Offences

The Tripartite is, in addition to the trade facilitation efforts above, also working on the development of legislation which will aid the exchange of information according to the

[123] The Comprehensive Trade and Transport Facilitation Programme (CTTFP) launched in 2011 is a series of initiatives from different RECs that have been brought together into one large integrated trade facilitation programme which includes: the NTB monitoring, reporting and removal system, border and customs procedures (one-stop border posts; integrated border Management, regional customs bond, transit management), immigration procedures, transport procedures (regional 3rd party insurance, vehicle standards and regulation, self-regulation of transporters, overload control, harmonised road user charges, regional corridor management systems and the establishment of the Joint Competition Authority linked to air transport liberalisation.

[124] COMESA-EAC-SADC Tripartite – Trade and transport facilitation: Focal Area 2 available at *http://www.comesa-eac-sadc-tripartite.org/intervention/focal_areas/trade_facilitation* (accessed 4 May 2013).

provisions of the Nairobi and Johannesburg Conventions to which most of the member states of the three REC's are members.

3.4 TARIFFS

The common external tariff of COMESA is harmonised with the common external tariff of the EAC. Effectively, this translates to the fact that the member states in both customs unions are not forced to choose which REC to remain in as both REC's adhere to the same common external tariff. In this manner COMESA and the EAC have managed to effectively address the dilemma of multiple memberships in terms of this specific aspect and have both moved closer towards becoming a single customs union.[125]

SADC however is still at the FTA stage of implementation having fallen behind on its Regional Indicative Strategic Development Plan (RISDP). The SADC FTA was launched in August 2008 and according to the SADC RISDP, a customs union was to be attained by 2010 however, due to capacity constraints within the SADC Secretariat, the implementation of the RISDP started late. At present the customs union has not yet been attained and there are currently 11 individual tariff policies which will need to be converged into a single and uniform tariff regime.[126]

3.5 CRITICAL ANALYSIS OF EFFORTS IN HARMONISATION

The TFTA will have to take into account separate legal and institutional arrangements and national frameworks for domesticating and implementing existing legal instruments on regional trade. Further, should the need arise for new TFTA institutions then cooperation structures and frameworks will require careful consideration and drafting. The TFTA negotiating principles state that the negotiations will build 'on the *acquis* of the existing REC FTA's.[127] The '*acquis'* theory is taken from European Union (EU) law and in terms of this,

---

[125]COMESA Customs Union: Brief on the COMESA Customs Union available at http://programmes.comesa.int/index.php?option=com_content&view=article&id=90&Itemid=142 (accessed 4 May 2013).

[126]Southern African Development Community: Customs Union Integration milestones available at http://www.sadc.int/about-sadc/integration-milestones/customs-union/ (accessed 4 May 2013).

[127]Hartzenberg T et al *The Tripartite Free Trade Area – Towards a new African Integration Paradigm?* (2012) 5.

the EU exercises supranational powers which the TFTA may well take cognisance of and aim to follow.

Overall, while there have been efforts at developing and adopting customs legislation and policies which are uniform across the TFTA region, more can be achieved still and there is ample scope for greater efforts in implementing the various agreements which have been signed by the member states of the TFTA. In fact, there have been customs audits conducted whose results reflect that there is slow progress in the implementation of both regional and international instruments and conventions by the customs administrations of member states.[128]

The results of the audit are important as they serve as a reflection of the state of affairs at the national level in terms of commitment to the development of the TFTA. The audit which was conducted by the Southern African Trade Hub was aimed at assessing the level of acceptance and implementation of the approved regional customs instruments and international conventions by the customs administrations of SADC member states. It was also an assessment of progress made in the harmonisation, standardisation and integration of the customs procedures, identifying areas of convergence and divergence, and an assessment of modernisation and trade facilitation levels and challenges.

The audit attributed the snail-pace progress to challenges and costs of multiple memberships by the member states to the three REC's among other factors. The results of the audit would be useful to the TFTA as a vital self assessment tool which would enable the REC secretariats to identify and target specific areas and issues which require attention in the area of harmonisation and standardisation of customs policies and procedures.

In addition and generally, although technical work has been performed in various working groups and a draft agreement with fourteen annexures prepared including, customs cooperation; simplification and harmonisation of trade documents and procedures; transit

[128] Technical Report: Audit of the Implementation of Regional SADC Customs Instruments and International Conventions Southern African Trade Hub October 2011 available at *http://www.satradehub.org/trade-facilitation/2011-audit-of-the-implementation-of-regional-sadc-customs-instruments-and-international-conventions/callelement*. (accessed 4 May 2013).

trade and transit facilities it must be admitted that there is still a mammoth task ahead before the TFTA achieves the dreams conceived at the first tripartite summit.[129]

Trade facilitation encompasses the systematic simplification and rationalisation of transparent, and simplified procedures and documentation for cross border trade. The proposed TFTA will inevitably result in increased trade volumes, and due to the complexity of global trade demands that customs procedures be kept simple, predictable and transparent to permit smooth flow of commerce as freely as possible, the tripartite is faced with the urgent need to develop institutional and regulatory reforms to customs procedures and behind-the-border measures.

Although Articles 13 to 15 of the TFTA annexure on trade facilitation provides for the simplification of customs procedures and facilitation and would ensure that the various TFTA regional projects on trade facilitation would proceed according to set targets, it however remains a stumbling block that the language which informs the said annexures fails to display a strong commitment to tackle these pertinent issues.

It could well be argued that the provisions within the annexures could be remedied with stricter compliance mechanisms which enable the supervision of the implementation of commitments and attract penalties for member states found to be deviating from the agreement. This strict compliance would then require supranational institutions to enforce such rules.

3.6 CONCLUSION

The challenge remains ahead to maintain the momentum attained by tripartite task force and its various cooperating partners especially when taking into consideration the complex operations of varying national regimes including rules and regulations, structures, resources, national development objectives, and addressing individual member countries' defensive trade interests.

---

[129] Otieno L. and Shinyekwa I 'Prospects and challenges in the formation of the COMESA-EAC-SADC Tripartite Free Trade Area' *Research Series 87 Economic Policy Research Centre* Nov. 2011 available at http://www.eprc.or.ug/pdf_files/series87.pdf (accessed 4 May 2013).

Political considerations have also negatively affected progress in the TFTA negotiations. Negotiations for the TFTA were launched in June 2011 to start with a six to 12 month preparatory phase and actual negotiations to commence in July 2012. Today however, the negotiations have lagged behind schedule by a year as member states deviate their focus to matters of leadership within the TFTA.[130]The challenge to policy makers and legislators in the TFTA therefore remains how to direct and drive the initiative to success on key policy issues and priorities in particular the sequencing of projects and restating and reaffirming desired outcomes.

It would not be amiss however, to argue that the successful harmonisation of existing legal frameworks could convey benefits in terms of the creation of a wider market for the business communities in the TFTA. This would promote competition and capitalise economies of scale for traders within the consolidated region. The economic integration agenda being implemented at the level of the three REC's has prioritised programmes which address trade facilitation challenges with the aim of lowering costs of doing business and improving the competitiveness of products from the region.[131]

These programmes encompass regulatory and policy reforms which support the adoption of international instruments and best practices; national and regional capacity building programmes to facilitate cross-border movements; and enhancement of infrastructure facilities at border posts to improve efficiency of cross-border movements.

In conclusion therefore, while the three REC's have achieved relative success in facilitating trade through the above programmes, there still remain major challenges of limited implementation and advancement of regional agreements at a national level including the requirements to implement different programmes and different instruments in countries that belong to more than one REC. there is also a need for the tripartite task force to provide guidance to member states and their international cooperating partners to in order to ensure harmonisation of the programmes of the REC's so that they complement each other rather

[130] Muwanga D, 'COMESA, SADC, EAC talks overdue' East African Business Week Monday, February 18th, 2013 available at *http://www.busiweek.com/index.php/the-eac-issues/eac-news/4517-comesa-sadc-eac-talks-overdue-* (accessed 4 May 2013).

[131] Nhara A 'Towards a Tripartite COMESA – EAC – SADC Free Trade Area: A panacea for deeper regional integration or a rhetoric African grouping' Trade and Development Studies Centre (2011) available at *http://cloud2.gdnet.org/cms.php?id=research_paper_abstract&research_paper_id=18275* (accessed 4 May 2013).

than compete against each other.[132] The tripartite task force has a huge task which it cannot ignore if the TFTA is to be a successful building block towards the pan-African vision of an African Economic Union.

[132] Kingombe C 'Lessons Learned from the Tripartite Free Trade Area' NEPAD Regional Integration and Trade Department (ONRI) African Development Bank Expert Group meeting on Preferential Trade Agreements and Regional Integration 5 December 2012 available at http://www.academia.edu/2243183/Lessons_Learned_from_the_Tripartite-Free_Trade_Area (accessed 4 May 2013).

CHAPTER 4: THE CUSTOMS UNION OF THE EUROPEAN UNION: DEVELOPMENT AND MODERNISATION

4.1 INTRODUCTION

This chapter seeks to explore and trace the development of the customs union (CU) of the European Union (EU) and how it has managed to achieve the deep level of legislative integration and technological cooperation which it boasts of today. The reason behind a specific assessment of the EU is the fact that as a regional grouping, it has managed to develop progressively to such a level that it is no longer a mere grouping of countries but has evolved and progressed to a deep level of integration such that it has supranational institutions with deep seated powers which have an impact even at a national level.[133]

The assessment is a critical one and aims to assist the Tripartite Free Trade Agreement (TFTA) member states to learn from EU experiences in developing harmonised customs legislation and how the member states of the EU have adopted and implemented the harmonised supranational legislation and technological framework for the single window. This chapter will also look at the EU single developments in terms of implementation time frames which should in turn assist the TFTA to gage its own time frames accord to a unique contextual framework which would apply specifically to the TFTA as a regional grouping still at a formative stage.

4.2 RATIONALE FOR A CUSTOMS UNION

Article XXIV of the General Agreement on Tariffs and Trade 1994 (GATT) sets out the conditions under which the formation of a free trade agreement (FTA) CU may be permitted. Through the enabling clause of the GATT, members of the World Trade Organisation (WTO) are permitted to 'accord differential and more favourable treatment to developing countries without according such treatment to other contracting parties.' It is on this basis that the CU of the EU derives its legitimacy. Through the aforementioned clauses, the EU was able to

[133] The European Court of Justice and the European Parliament are some examples of the supranational institutions. Also see Fontaine P. *Europe in 12 lessons* European Commission (2006) available at http://ec.europa.eu/archives/publications/booklets/eu_glance/60/en.pdf (accessed 4 May 2013).

create a CU which would be used as an engine for deeper economic integration and create economies of scale for industries operating within its regional economic space to its advantage.

CU's are often pursued by states in a bid to attain a myriad of objectives, including the creation of regional public goods such as security or democracy. This was indeed the case for the EU[134]. Robert Schuman and Jean Monnet[135] were unambiguous that the purpose of the European Coal and Steel Community (ECSC), which was the precursor of the European Economic Community (EEC) and eventually the EU, was to make Franco-German war not only 'unthinkable, but materially impossible.'[136] In fact, the preamble to the Treaty of Paris 'resolved to substitute for age-old rivalries the merging of their essential interests; [and] to create, by establishing an economic community, the basis for a broader and deeper community among peoples long divided by bloody conflicts.'

Further echoes in support of this view are further elucidated by Dr. Hallstein[137] who stated that: 'We are not in business at all; we are in politics'[138] In actual fact, a CU can gradually evolve and progress to become a deeper alliance over time, exhibiting such features as a common market, the harmonisation of regulations and standards, and development of supranational institutions as in the case of the EU.[139]

Another important factor which advocates the formation of a CU between neighbours is the potential economic benefit which a CU may produce as a result of the shrinkage of the costs of trade which are concerned with numerous border formalities. Often, these hidden costs of trade pose as greater hindrances to trade than actual customs duties and are in all probability

---

[134] Urwin D, *Community of Europe: A history of European Integration since 1945* (1995) 3.

[135] The founding fathers, so to speak, of the EU. On the 9th of May 1950, France approached its European partners to propose the creation of the European Coal and Steel Community (ECSC), the forerunner of today's European Union. This proposal is known as "the Schuman declaration" however, the idea originally belonged to Jean Monnet though it was Robert Schuman, who set it in motion.

[136] Pietrzyk M, *International order and individual liberty: Effects of war and peace on the development of governments* (2002) 167.

[137] Walter Hallstein was EU Commission President from 1958 to 1967 available at *http://www4.dr-rath-foundation.org/brussels_eu/who_is_who/index.html* (accessed 4 May 2013).

[138] Ganz R, Hallstein Notes Political Goals of Common Market available at, *http://www.thecrimson.com/article/1961/5/23/hallstein-notes-political-goals-of-common/* (accessed 4 May 2013).

[139] Mongelli F et al, 'What does European institutional integration tell us about trade integration?' *Occasional Paper Series No. 40* (2005) European Central Bank available at *http://www.ecb.int/pub/pdf/scpops/ecbocp40.pdf* (accessed 4 May 2013).

more easily avoidable between adjacent states than among states which are far-flung from each other.[140] Even for neighbouring states however, the elimination of these costs could easily become a complex and expensive process. This is the reason why the creation of a CU for the EU was a protracted process for the EU taking up to approximately 33 years from 1957 until the mid-1990's to advance towards the stage of achieving 'invisible borders' between even a subset of its member states.[141]

While *prima facie* CU's may be more appealing in comparison to FTA's, this is however only where the internal borders of the CU are effectively abolished and a low common external tariff is applied. It is also paramount that the institutions which are created by a CU for the development of trade policy should be backed by political will. This is in addition to the fact that they should be structured in such a way that a single regional authority is charged with the responsibility of developing policies which are directed towards effective and progressive removal of trade barriers and developing a common regional legislative framework for customs and reduction of trade barriers if the CU is to be of any benefit to its members.

4.3 ACHIEVEMENT OF A CUSTOMS UNION IN THE EUROPEAN UNION

The creation of the CU of the EU became a reality when on the 1st of July 1968[142], the member countries of the then EEC agreed to the total removal of customs duties between member states. Counting from the date of the momentous decision to remove customs duties to the present day, the CU of the EU is currently in its 45th year of existence, with an ever important role and is an integral part of the very foundations of the EU. From its inception the CU has experienced a sustained rate of rapid economic growth and has evolved in its expansion from an initial membership of six states to up to the current membership to date of 27 member states. Along with the initial progressive act of the removal of customs duties

---

[140] 'The costs and benefits of trade facilitation' OECD Policy Brief October 2005 available at http://www.mincomes.it/semproitalia/tavolo_strategico/8_documenti/OCSE/OCSE/Contenuti/Cost%20Benefits%20of%20Trade%20Facilitation.pdf (accessed 4 May 2013).

[141] Borchardt K, 'The ABC of European Union law' European Union (2010) available at http://europa.eu/documentation/legislation/pdf/oa8107147_en.pdf (accessed 4 May 2013).

[142] Treaty establishing the European Economic Community (TEEC) 1957. This agreement led to the founding of the European Economic Community on 1 January 1958. This treaty was signed on 25 March 1957 by Belgium, France, Italy, Luxembourg, the Netherlands and West Germany. It set out the four economic freedoms that it wanted to create in Europe which include the free movement of goods which was established with the creation of the European Customs Union in 1968.

amongst member states, subsequently, the EU has since then instituted several incremental common customs policies for the member states of the EU.[143]

The CU of the EU can arguably be said to be both the culmination of as well as a product of political will coupled together with the realisation that deeper economic regional integration is the key driver to achieving and maintaining a competitive presence in the global trading environment.[144] The discussions surrounding the proposals for creating a European CU were first introduced in view of the ECSC which was founded through the Treaty of Paris.[145]

In terms of the Treaty of Paris, the envisaged regional economic community (REC) would be established on the premises that a common market would be created, which market would cover coal and steel as these were the primary materials at the time needed to drive the industrialisation in Europe.[146] It is however the Treaty of Rome which enabled the establishment of a European common market and is the basis upon which the CU of the EU was eventually established. This treaty was founded on the principle that there would be an EEC. It is the EEC together with the completion of the single market as envisaged in terms of the Single European Act (SEA)[147]which would be the precursor of the EU; which was then subsequently established in 1993 through the Treaty of Maastricht.[148]

With the creation of the CU, the Treaty of Rome brought about the removal of customs barriers within the EEC and also established a common customs tariff which would be applicable to all goods which originated from countries which did not form part of the EEC. From the beginning, the major economic principles of the CU of the EU have been directed at the removal of all forms of customs duties at internal borders between EU member states and

[143] Fontaine P. *Europe in 12 lessons* European Commission (2006) available at http://ec.europa.eu/archives/publications/booklets/eu_glance/60/en.pdf (accessed 4 May 2013).
[144] Pietrzyk M, *International order and individual liberty: Effects of war and peace on the development of governments* (2002) 167.
[145] Treaty establishing the European Coal and Steel Community, 1951 which subsequently became the European Union.
[146]Communication From The Commission To The Council, The European Parliament And The European Economic And Social Committee Strategy For The Evolution Of The Customs Union. Com (2008) 169_en) available at http://ec.europa.eu/taxation_customs/resources/documents/customs/com(2008)169_en.pdf (accessed 4 May 2013).
[147] The Single European Act (SEA) was the first significant revision of the Treaty of Rome .It established the objective of establishing a single market by 31 December 1992.
[148] The Treaty on European Union (TEU) was signed on 7 February 1992. Upon its entry into force on 1 November 1993 it created the European Union. The Maastricht Treaty has been amended by the treaties of Amsterdam, Nice and Lisbon.

in turn, the establishment of common customs tariffs on imports from outside of the EU. Its other principles include the drive towards imposing common customs duties on imports from outside the EU, establishing common rules of origin for products from outside the EU and arriving at a common definition of customs value among member states.[149]

It can be argued that for a CU to be able to function effectively there has to be a common policy approach to the application of rules at external borders by member states. This argument therefore dictates that all the national customs administrations of the member states of the EU must, as of necessity, act in unison as if they were one single administration. It also demands that these common rules extend beyond the confines of the CU agreement to encompass all other aspects of trade policy measures.[150]

To add to the above, part of the establishment of a CU requires the removal or rationalisation of non-tariff barriers and this cannot be said to be a straightforward exercise. The harmonisation of non-tariff barriers is an onerous requirement, for example for the first 30 years, the EU permitted its member states to maintain their own quotas on certain third-country imports such as clothing, footwear, and steel and to compensate with the use of border measures to prevent those goods from crossing internal borders within the EU. This ostensibly illustrates that a CU effectively demands a clear and common trade policy in addition to requiring a common external tariff (CET).

Since the initial conception of the CU, the EU has remained dynamic in its development and this has directly allowed for EU customs administrations to continue to play a pivotal trade facilitation role within an increasingly challenging global trading environment. In addition, the EU also embarked on a modernisation drive aimed at reforming and streamlining customs.[151] As part of this modernisation programme, the EU legal environment was modernised with the issuing of the modernised customs code. Broadly defined, today the

[149] Borchardt K, 'The ABC of European Union law' European Union (2010) available at http://europa.eu/documentation/legislation/pdf/oa8107147_en.pdf (accessed 4 May 2013).

[150] In a scenario where the policies of a CU are enshrined within the founding document or constitution for example as in the case of the EU's Treaty of Rome, or in the case where a CU creates its own bureaucratic institutions or structures which are legitimised and can be defended, it becomes difficult for member states to renege from the constitution or founding document or follow rogue domestic policies which do not conform to the common goals of the CU.

[151] 'Trade policies and practices by measure' WTO Trade Policy Review available at http://www.wto.org/english/tratop_e/tpr_e/s214-03_e.doc (accessed 4 May 2013).

directive of the CU is to function as a single customs territory which applies common customs legislation for the entire EU regional economic community in a standardised manner. Its goals are directed towards facilitating legitimate trade, applying a single customs policy effectively, and the protection of European society.[152]

In addition to the abovementioned efforts at modernisation, a European Parliament and council decision was implemented which was singularly directed at the creation of a pan-European electronic customs system. This system is essentially aimed towards the creation of a paperless environment for customs and trade and supports a solid communication chain between all customs authorities within the EU and other governmental authorities operating at the border, and between governmental authorities and traders.[153]

The CU is an integral pillar of the EU and it is also vital to the successful performance of the European single market which was fully established in 1993. The EU today is undeniably an extensive regional market on a colossal scale and as such can only function effectively in the existence of a strong regional policy and a common application of uniform rules at its external borders. As a result thereof, the CU has enabled the EU to direct its efforts toward two goals[154] which are firstly, towards the facilitation of trade and secondly, towards protection of the interests of the citizens of EU member states.

As previously stated above, two remarkable achievements of the customs union of the EU have been the creation of a common customs tariff and a common customs code. The common customs tariff is applicable to goods which are imported across the external borders of the EU. The legal framework for this code was established in 1992. As a result of this, today, the national customs services of the EU member states now cooperate with each other

[152] Borchardt K, 'The ABC of European Union law' European Union (2010) available at http://europa.eu/documentation/legislation/pdf/oa8107147_en.pdf (accessed 4 May 2013).
[153] Communication From The Commission To The Council, The European Parliament And The European Economic And Social Committee Strategy For The Evolution Of The Customs Union. Com (2008) 169_en) available at http://ec.europa.eu/taxation_customs/resources/documents/customs/com(2008)169_en.pdf (last accessed 3 April 2013).
[154] Borchardt K, 'The ABC of European Union law' European Union (2010) available at http://europa.eu/documentation/legislation/pdf/oa8107147_en.pdf (accessed 4 May 2013).

to effectively act as a single common customs service through the application of common customs legislation and working methods.[155]

4.4 A MODERNISED CUSTOMS CODE FOR THE EUROPEAN UNION

The community customs code is part of the ongoing strategy for the evolution of the CU legal framework[156] and came into effect in April of 2008. This modernised customs code was developed as part of an evolutionary adaptation strategy in order that the economy of the EU could continue to compete effectively and maintain a strong presence within the global trading environment, in addition, it was developed in light of the need to enable the national customs ICT systems of the EU member states to exchange electronic information based on commonly used technology.[157]

The modernisation and simplification of the entire EU customs legal and technological environment began with a significant amendment to the then community customs code[158] of the European Parliament and of the European Council which amended council regulation (EEC) No 2913/92 establishing the community customs code which was adopted in 2005. These amendments conferred on EU customs authorities the powers to apply highly sophisticated security controls in customs, whilst simultaneously developing an environment which would not disrupt legitimate trade.[159]

---

[155] 'Trade policies and practices by measure' WTO Trade Policy Review available at http://www.wto.org/english/tratop_e/tpr_e/s214-03_e.doc (accessed 4 May 2013).

[156] Regulation (EC) No 450/2008 of the European Parliament and of the Council of 23 April 2008 laying down the Community Customs Code (The modernized Customs Code) OJ L 145, 4.6.2008. This Code was aimed at the adaptation of customs legislation to fit, but also to govern, the electronic environment for customs and trade. This regulation entered into force on 24 June 2008, but it is not yet applicable. It is due to be applicable once its implementing provisions are in force and on 24 June 2013 at the latest available at http://eur-lex.europa.eu/LexUriServ/LexUriServ.do?uri=OJ:L:2008:145:0001:0064:En:PDF (accessed 4 May 2013).

[157] Electronic Customs Multi-Annual Strategic Plan: 2008 Yearly Revision (MASP) European Commission Directorate-General Taxation and Customs Union available at http://ec.europa.eu/taxation_customs/resources/documents/customs/policy_issues/e-customs_initiative/MASP_strategic_plan_en.pdf (accessed 20 April 2013).

[158] Regulation (EC) No 648/2005 of The European Parliament and of the Council of 13 April 2005 amending Council Regulation (EEC) No 2913/92 establishing the Community Customs Code http://eur-lex.europa.eu/LexUriServ/LexUriServ.do?uri=CELEX:32005R0648:en:HTML (accessed 4 May 2013).

[159] Communication From The Commission To The Council, The European Parliament And The European Economic And Social Committee Strategy For The Evolution Of The Customs Union. Com (2008) 169_en) available at http://ec.europa.eu/taxation_customs/resources/documents/customs/com(2008)169_en.pdf (accessed 4 May 2013).

The modernised customs code was developed with the view that it would enable the implementation of the simplification of processes essential to enhancing customs and trade in order that they work cheaper and more efficiently. The electronic customs decision which complements the modernised customs code also represents a significant move through enabling the linkage of national customs ICT systems of member states within the EU to the advantage of both customs and trade. As a consequence thereof, the resultant pan-European electronic customs system will manage to increase the competitiveness of companies trading within the EU space through the reduction of compliance costs and better security at EU borders. In addition, the creation of a single market for the CU has translated into the fact that customs formalities at borders between member states are also now a thing of the past.[160]

From the above, it becomes clear that the EU modern customs code is progressive in that it establishes the competencies of the national customs authorities, provides overall concordance in customs procedures, aids in making procedures more predictable and transparent, promotes cooperation governments and the private sector, and provides a framework for legal recourse procedures.

In addition, as a result of the current level of interconnectivity which already exists between the national customs authorities in the EU, there is ample information with regards to the movement of all goods imported into or exported from the EU through the application of sophisticated customs electronic systems and methods to control all types of goods. This is regardless of the fact that the volumes of goods movements across the external borders of the EU are enormous.[161]

Moreover, as a direct consequence of the rapidly dynamic environment within which customs operates in, the customs authority of the EU has been charged with the central responsibility of ensuring that the equilibrium between the need to protect society and facilitating trade

---

[160] Communication From The Commission To The Council, The European Parliament And The European Economic And Social Committee Strategy For The Evolution Of The Customs Union. Com (2008) 169_en) available at http://ec.europa.eu/taxation_customs/resources/documents/customs/com(2008)169_en.pdf (accessed 4 May 2013).

[161] Puggliatti L, 'Cloud single window: legal implications of a new model of cross-border single window' (2011) 5 *WCJ* 13 available at http://www.worldcustomsjournal.org/media/wcj/-2011/2/Pugliatti.pdf (accessed 4 May 2013).

through the control of the supply chain, at the external borders as well as within the EU is maintained at all times.[162]

4.5 ORIGINAL AND FUTURE SUCCESSES – IN INFORMATION AND COMMUNICATIONS TECHNOLOGY

The amendment of the customs code has also witnessed the streamlining and subsequent improvement of the planned EU-wide customs IT system and further enhanced regional capacity towards combating fraud in the customs sector.[163] Enshrined in the provisions of the customs code is an enhanced undertaking for EU customs and in terms of this enhanced undertaking, the application of ICT is singled out as being essential to the successful integration and interconnection of national customs procedures throughout the EU.

These are important legal and technological strides which have equipped EU customs both for the medium term and long term future.[164] Furthermore, in a bid to enhance the interoperability between member states' automated customs systems, the European Council and the European Parliament adopted a decision on a paperless environment for customs and trade.

In order for the economy of the EU to continue competing globally, it was essential for the various national customs ICT systems of the member states to possess the ability to exchange electronic information amongst themselves and with traders through various interfaces based on commonly used technology. In view of this need, the mandate to create and operate a trans-European customs system required a legal basis for the possible use of electronic declarations. Therefore, a major initiative for the EU customs union, in the development of

---

[162] Borchardt K, 'The ABC of European Union law' European Union (2010) available at *http://europa.eu/documentation/legislation/pdf/oa8107147_en.pdf* (accessed 4 May 2013).

[163] Communication from the Commission to the European Parliament, the Council, and the European Economic and social committee on the state of the customs union Brussels (2012) available at *http://ec.europa.eu/taxation_customs/resources/documents/common/publications/com_reports/customs/com(2012)791_en.pdf* (accessed 4 May 2013).

[164] EU Commission staff working paper (The 1996 Single Market Review: Background Information for the Report to the Council available at *http://ec.europa.eu/internal_market/economic-reports/docs/bkground_en.pdf* (accessed 4 May 2013).

electronic customs had its direction and substance governed by joint decisions, and a common code of practice.[165]

Developments in ICT for customs have been inextricably intertwined with the evolution of policy, legislation, and procedures in the EU customs union. In the beginning, ICT was an area of national preserve and exclusive national competence. In terms of this nationalistic construct, ICT systems were initially designed to cater for the operational responsibilities of individual member states. Subsequent to this however, in the spirit of regional integration and connectivity, ICT solutions known as customs trans-European electronic systems were developed.

As stated earlier, the CU is in a state of continual evolution and improvement and as such one of the programmes driving the improvement of electronic customs in the EU is the Customs 2013 work programme.[166] In terms of this regional initiative, key areas in electronic customs are identified as priorities for investment and development. Once an area has been earmarked for development, it must subsequently be approved by the member states of the EU and thereafter the same development and implementation of the programme is then monitored through regular meetings of a Customs 2013 committee.[167]

4.5.1 The Single Administrative Document

In the EU, the single administrative document (SAD) is used within the framework of trade with third countries and in order to facilitate the movement of non-EU goods within the EU. Even then, it is applicable only in extremely restricted cases. The SAD is aimed at ensuring openness in national administrative requirements, rationalise and reduce administrative documentation, reduce the amount of requested information and standardise and harmonise

[165] Regulation (EC) No 450/2008 of the European Parliament and of the Council of 23 April 2008 laying down the Community Customs Code (The modernized Customs Code) OJ L 145, 4.6.2008 available at *http://eur-lex.europa.eu/LexUriServ/LexUriServ.do?uri=OJ:L:2008:145:0001:0064:En:PDF* (accessed 4 May 2013).
[166] DG Taxation and Customs Union Management Plan 2012 available at *http://ec.europa.eu/atwork/synthesis/amp/doc/taxud_mp.pdf* (accessed 4 May 2013).
[167] DG Taxation and Customs Union Management Plan 2012 available at *http://ec.europa.eu/atwork/synthesis/amp/doc/taxud_mp.pdf* (accessed 4 May 2013).

data. It applies in instances where goods are required to be placed under any form of customs procedure but where a computerised electronic system has not yet been implemented.[168]

The SAD introduction was made simultaneously with concomitant SAD legislation which was required to enable optimum adaptation of the EU-wide customs service to the needs of the global trading environment. Regulation 2286/2003 enabled this adaption through the introduction of a radical modernisation of data collection processes with regards to customs declarations.

The EU adopted the SAD in 1988 and as a result thereof, the majority of its member states managed to simplify their customs procedures, significantly reducing customs hurdles for traders. Despite this progress however, it has been estimated that during the early 1990's period the costs of border formalities affecting intra-EU trade, which trade was already mostly duty free except for some goods originating from Portugal and Spain, were equivalent to more than 1.2 percent of the gross value of internally traded goods.[169]

The concept of the SAD was initially developed as a starting point towards the removal of customs formalities in intra-EU trade. Today, the SAD has almost been eliminated in the context of the technological advances which have been made in developing electronic customs systems across the EU.[170] The SAD is therefore a relic of a pre-computerisation customs system but works well nevertheless in conjunction with the modern customs code without compromising the development of computerised procedures. It remains an important aid and will most probably remain to play a role in the continued simplification and harmonisation of customs procedures.

---

[168] 'The single administrative document' European Commission: Taxation and Customs Union available at http://ec.europa.eu/taxation_customs/customs/procedural_aspects/general/sad/ (accessed 4 May 2013).

[169] EU Commission staff working paper (The 1996 Single Market Review: Background Information for the Report to the Council. Available at http://ec.europa.eu/internal_market/economic-reports/docs/bkground_en.pdf (accessed 4 May 2013).

[170] 'New customs transit systems for Europe' prepared by the office for official publications of the European Communities (2001) available at http://ec.europa.eu/taxation_customs/resources/documents/annex_i_transit_brochure_en.pdf (accessed 4 May 2013).

4.6 RECOMMENDATIONS FOR THE TFTA FROM EU EXPERIENCES

The CU of the EU is a strong pillar as elucidated above and it continues to play a pivotal role in maintaining the strong global trading position which the EU commands today in the world trading arena. The evolution of the EU and its CU is not final and it keeps changing to meet the revolving dynamics of the trading environment its member states operate within.

Any agreed CU designs, principles, policies, and procedures must be anchored in a legal instrument. This stems from the fact that any major goal of a CU is to ensure that there is a uniform and consistent application of union rules and in this regard, a common enabling framework promotes the attainment of such a goal. A customs code should therefore be able to effectively provide a solid framework for modern and efficient operations which in turn must be in conformity with the broad dictates of such a code.

One option for the evolution of the Tripartite Free Trade Agreement (TFTA) would be to develop a common customs code, as the EU did in 1992. In addition, the process of adopting a harmonised legal framework for customs can well serve as vehicle for simplification, and modernisation which is aligned to the international principles of the World Customs Organisation.

From the perspective of the TFTA member states, the proposition of market integration is both a sensible and attractive choice as it is critical for the region's economic development further to this, market integration will secure much needed economic growth and increased trade volumes through the creation of a cohesive investment area and the evolution of the TFTA into a customs union. With deeper integration, the small currently fragmented economies in the TFTA region could stand to gain from a larger economic space and allow comparative advantages among regional industries to play out to the advantage of the region as a whole.

It is undeniable that FTA's are less burdensome to create and can be institutionally uncomplicated, whereas customs unions demand the negotiation of a common external tariff and coordination of all future trade policy changes for the entire REC.[171] This relative ease of creation of the FTA model in regional integration could well be a distraction from the real need behind the reason for constructing a CU model rather than focusing on the demands of creation.

It is at such a crucial point in deciding the future direction that political will and unity of resolve is required for the member states to push the evolution of the TFTA into becoming a CU. A further important distinction is that between FTA's and CU's, the latter, in addition to possessing the internal free trade characteristic of FTA's, also include a common trade policy toward third countries.[172] This in turn translates to the loss of a relative amount of sovereignty in order to allow a supranational economic state of affairs.[173]

In light of this vision of economic growth and deeper integration, the TFTA may well borrow a leaf or two from the successful development of the EU in becoming a CU. The CU has contributed immensely to achieving economic successes of mammoth proportions by facilitating trade within the union and with external countries. Today, the EU can safely boast of having the largest trading space in the world with a population of over 490 million people.[174]

A REC which had its genesis in political ambition has evolved spectacularly to becoming a unique economic community with supranational powers. The European Union has become today a regional economic community whose focus is on economic growth. This is a far cry from its origins in the ECSC whose conception was based on political ambition more than economic integration of the European region.

Its development and success has demanded deeper integration, closer policy structuring and a relative loss of sovereignty for its members. These are hard facts which the TFTA has to live

---

[171] Chauffour J and Maur J (eds) *Preferential Trade Agreement Policies for Development: A Handbook*, edited by Jean-Pierre (2011) 113-4.

[172] Lasok D, *The trade and customs law of the European Union (1998)* 3.

[173] Evans D 'Options for Regional Integration in Southern Africa' *IDS Working Paper* 94 7 available at *http://acp-eu-trade.org/library/files/EVANS_IDS_wp94_2001_options%20for%20RI%20in%20Sthn%20Africa.pdf* (accessed 25 April 2013).

[174] What is the European Union? Available at *http://eeas.europa.eu/delegations/new_zealand/eu_new_zealand/political_economics_relations/agreements/faq/index_en.htm* (last accessed 13 March 2013).

with should it consider following the beaten path which has been forged by the EU. The resultant effect of deeper integration is the creation of a single market which has the potential for massive economic benefits therefore; the development of the TFTA into a customs union will be a sure way to secure a paradigm shift from a poor economic outlook to unlocking exponential growth.

As a result, Africa will no longer stand as a peripheral participant on the global trading field but will become transformed into an economic powerhouse and force to be acknowledged. Through the unlocking of economic potential through the harmonisation of customs procedures using law and technology, the TFTA, and Africa will gain a stronger negotiating and vantage point for better trade terms which suit Africa's bespoke needs in trade development.

In conclusion, the EU has demonstrated that the process of regional integration through harmonisation of legislation and technology (the single window in this case) is not an easy one but rather one which demands time and commitment from all member countries involved. It also demands that a REC develops or progresses from one initially being an FTA and adheres to common deeper integration policies aimed at unifying different national policies in respect of a particular economic focal area, in this specific case, customs. It is to be expected that the TFTA member states will gradually etch closer towards considering the option of deeper regional integration and in the event that the initial free trade area (FTA) concept successfully actualises, it should form part of the normal progression and evolution of the TFTA that there will be gravitation from the initial free trade arrangement towards eventual transformation into a CU like the EU.

CHAPTER 5: DEVELOPING A LEGAL AND ICT FRAMEWORK FOR THE TFTA REGIONAL SINGLE WINDOW.

5.1 INTRODUCTION

This chapter builds on the previous chapters by adopting a composite perspective whereby proposals are advanced for the approach to be followed when designing a legal and technological framework for customs specifically with the Tripartite Free Trade Agreement (TFTA) in mind. Through an assessment of the various approaches which are adopted in developing a legal and technological framework for the TFTA, it will become possible to gain a better understanding of the type of legal framework which would be best suited to the TFTA in addition to identifying the best design for a customs processing system which would serve the TFTA countries optimally whilst allowing room for national and regional separation in terms of implementation of the system once it is in place.

The World Customs Organization (WCO) and the United Nations (UN)[175] have time and again advocated for the adoption of the single window through promoting awareness of the economic benefits of single window customs processing system.[176] While using Information and Communications Technology (ICT) is certainly not the only existent methodology for the development of a single window, an ICT approach has nevertheless been afforded prominence especially by the WCO through the Revised Kyoto Convention.[177] Additionally, the exponential proliferation of electronic commerce transactions in international business trade has substantiated the increase in the significance of ICT as a basis for the development of single window operations.[178]

---

[175] Recommendation 33 – *Recommendation and Guidelines on Establishing a Single Window*, July 2005, United Nations Centre for Trade Facilitation and Electronic Business UNCEFACT (2005) available at www.unece.org/cefact/recommendations/rec35/Rec35-PublicReviewDraftv9-Feb09.doc (accessed 3 April 2013); Recommendation 35 – *Establishing a legal framework for international trade Single Window*, October 2010, UNCEFACT (2010) available at www.unece.org/cefact/recommendations/rec35/Rec35-PublicReviewDraftv9-Feb09.doc (accessed 3 April 2013).

[176] The WCO Data model: Single Window Data Harmonisation, Version 2, February 2007 WCO (2007) available at http://www.wcoomd.org/sw_guidelines.htm (accessed 3 April 2013).

[177] International Convention on the Simplification and Harmonization of Customs Procedures, *as amended* (1999) the revised Kyoto Convention, developed by the World Customs Organization entered into force on February 3, 2006.

[178] Luddy W. 'Single Window and Paperless Trade Legal Issues: A Possible Mosaic' Global Trade Facilitation Conference 2011 available at

In response to these august calls, most progressive customs administrations globally, in partnership with their accompanying border agencies and trade partners, have so far made various efforts to establish single window processing systems in their jurisdictions. In this regard, it is acknowledged that the construction of a single window system, and more so a regional single window is one of mammoth proportions, entailing in depth strategic planning coupled with the optimal use of information technology, adequate financial backing together with competent human resources and most importantly, the requisite political support to drive the process.[179]

The World Trade Organisation (WTO) also recognises that successful efforts at trade facilitation result in a mutually beneficial economic relationship for all parties involved.[180] As a direct consequence thereof, trade facilitation was incorporated into the Doha round of multilateral trade negotiations, thereby projecting and conveying a message across of a strong sense of international consensus with regards to the importance of trade facilitation in enhancing economic development and trade competitiveness.[181]

As part of this consensus, the Doha negotiations included the aim to clarify and improve on certain aspects of Articles V, VIII, and X of the General Agreement on Tariffs and Trade 1994 (GATT) which relate to the freedom of transit, fees and formalities connected with importation and exportation, the publication and administration of trade regulations respectively, with a view to further improving on the movement, release and clearance of goods, including goods in transit.[182] In this respect, the proposed regional single window for the TFTA, as a trade facilitation tool, will assist in the abovementioned aims of improving on the movement, release and clearance of goods within the TFTA.

---

http://www.unece.org/fileadmin/DAM/trade/Trade_Facilitation_Forum/ConferencePPTs/D02_08AM_BillLuddy.pdf. (accessed 4 April 2013).

[179] Butterly T, 'UNECE Recommendations, Standards and tools for International Trade Single Window' *United Nations Economic Commission for Europe (UNECE)* available at http://css.escwa.org.lb/edgd/1476/d1s1-2.pdf (accessed 4 April 2013).

[180] Andrew Grainger 'Trade Facilitation: A Review' *Trade Facilitation Working Paper* 25 June 2007 available at www.tradefacilitation.co.uk (accessed 3 April 2013).

[181] Doha development agenda: Doha Work programme WTO available at http://www.wto.org/english/tratop_e/dda_e/draft_text_gc_dg_31july04_e.htm (accessed 3 April 2013).

[182] WTO Briefing notes on Doha agenda and trade facilitation available at http://www.wto.org/english/tratop_e/dda_e/status_e/tradfa_e.htm (accessed 3 April 2013).

The above aspects are integral to the trade facilitation agenda, especially Article VIII (1)(c) which enjoins contracting parties to the GATT to work towards minimising the incidence and complexity of import and export formalities and for decreasing and simplifying import and export documentation requirements.[183] This is especially important in relation to the members of the TFTA who also need to ensure that any regional arrangements they enter into are compliant with the prescripts of the GATT.

In the same vein, the lack of consensus at the multilateral level should not typify a standstill for the TFTA member states who may still, nevertheless formulate bilateral attempts to achieve some of the Doha goals, within a regional economic community setting and through alternative approaches, one of which would be that of creating a regional single window for the TFTA region. The development of this single window for the TFTA region will also as of necessity, include the drafting of a TFTA regional customs protocol which will form the basic framework upon which national legislations will correspondingly be structured and aligned to reflect the regional customs protocol.

From the aforegoing, it becomes necessary to focus on the planning and requirements which are demanded for the development and implementation of a single window processing system on a regional scale for the TFTA. A number of factors will have to be considered when seeking to turn the single window regional endeavour a success and these will be addressed below. These include such considerations as managing the transition from theory to actual implementation and the courting of stakeholders to partner the process financially and in terms of technical support.

5.2 PLANNING, PREPARATION AND IMPLEMENTATION OF THE SINGLE WINDOW

Once the concept of a single window has been approved, the next step is that of developing the same concept to its actual materialisation. The primary hurdle to be faced, or rather one of the challenges faced by the TFTA member countries is that of developing the concept of a regional single window created through the interlinking of uniform national single windows

[183] De Wulf L and Sokol J, B *Customs Modernization Handbook* (2005) 52.

using cloud technology; through to the reality of actualisation and becoming a fully operational system which is used by the customs administrations within the TFTA.

To achieve a functional regional single window for the TFTA, the member countries would have to align and develop national single windows which are compatible and interlinked within the TFTA region thereby enabling the efficient interaction of customs administrations across the TFTA and allowing exchange of information.[184] Conformity to international data standards in import and export is vital to the success of the regional single window system. In this sense, the WCO data model[185] if applied can help ensure compatibility and interoperability among customs administrations.

It is therefore relevant to embark on a discussion of the following aspects which are pertinent to address before embarking on a project of such proportions. It is essential in the sense that any project requires funding and support and any envisaged project must be well thought out and any risks or challenges identified beforehand if the planned project will stand any chances of being a success. These three factors are; the courting of stakeholders of the single window and its single users, the formulation of a suitable design for the single window and finally, the obstacles which will be faced in all probability during the design and implementation phases.

5.2.1 Courting stakeholders and potential users of the single window

In addition to this, member countries will also have to conscientise their relevant ministries and agencies, which would include the customs administrations, ministries of trade, finance, and other relevant ministries, *a propos* the importance of establishing such a single window in order to secure cooperation amongst these entities in the development of the national single windows.[186] When developing a system which will be used by the government and the

---

[184] Puggliatti L, 'Cloud single window: legal implications of a new model of cross-border single window' (2011) 5 *WCJ* 13 available at *http://www.worldcustomsjournal.org/media/wcj/-2011/2/Pugliatti.pdf* (accessed 4 May 2013).

[185] The WCO Data model: Single Window Data Harmonisation, Version 2, February 2007 WCO (2007) available at *http://www.wcoomd.org/sw_guidelines.htm* (accessed 3 April 2013).

[186] Ponten J, 'Single window – best practice and the way forward' Discussion paper *UNCITRAL colloquium on electronic commerce* New York, USA, February 14-16th 2011 available at *http://www.uncitral.org/pdf/english/colloquia/EC/Ponten_SW_Best_Practice_and_the_Way_Forward.pdf* (accessed 4 May 2013).

private sector, it would be also advisable to also ensure that the private sector is fully involved, advised and consulted during the planning and developmental phase.[187] The global concepts of international trade, the need for shared intelligence, integrated border management, and need for coupling national efficiencies due to shrinking resources, makes partnerships between private and public sector agencies imperative.[188] A private-public-partnership in the development of a single window could also alleviate the challenge of financing as governments are often cash strapped with limited resources.

A partnership of this nature is central to successful trade facilitation efforts and requires the existence of a structured dialogue schema and collaborative capacity building and training on both sides of the partnership arrangement. This alliance will permit all parties (including the staff who will use the system) involved to possess a sense of ownership of the single window system and obtain a better understanding of the working of the processing system.[189] This sense of ownership over the single window will also be heightened in the presence of a common vision. This is also essential for all the agencies and ministries which will be involved in the development of the single interoperable customs systems to cooperate meaningfully and easily accept and implement the corresponding customs legislation to be implemented.[190]

As the external borders of a country are characteristically the initial and most integral point of interaction between trade and governance and this would be the most appropriate place of implementation of the single window interface between government and trade and for the interconnectivity required to enable the regional single window system. The proper implementation of a national single window system especially at national borders will then contribute significantly towards easing trade constraints at internal borders of the TFTA

[187] Kyoto Convention guidelines on the application of information and communication technology by the World Customs Organisation June 2004 at page 11, available at http://www.insw.go.id/images/public/kyoto-ict-guidelines-wco.pdf (accessed 3 April 2013).

[188] Key Factors in Establishing Single Windows for Handling Import/Export Procedures and Formalities: Trade Facilitation and the Single Window E/ESCWA/EDGD/2011/5 10 November 2011 at 27 available at http://www.wto.org/english/tratop_e/tradfa_e/case_studies_e/escwa_e.pdf (accessed 3 April 2013).

[189] Kyoto Convention guidelines on the application of information and communication technology by the World Customs Organisation June 2004 at 25 available at http://www.insw.go.id/images/public/kyoto-ict-guidelines-wco.pdf (accessed 3 April 2013).

[190] Ponten J, 'Single window – best practice and the way forward' Discussion paper *UNCITRAL colloquium on electronic commerce* New York, USA, February 14-16th 2011 available at http://www.uncitral.org/pdf/english/colloquia/EC/Ponten_SW_Best_Practice_and_the_Way_Forward.pdf (accessed 4 May 2013).

region, simultaneously reducing a significant percentage of non-tariff barriers to trade in the TFTA region.[191]

5.2.2 Formulating the design of the single window model.

In addition, an ideal, single window would be one that makes regulatory requirements accessible to the trading community at one point effectively accelerating the clearance process. To make this a success however, this information sharing scenario has to extend to all regulations by all relevant agencies. Therefore, the trading community should have access to requisite information from all other government agencies.[192]This is an important consideration in that the development of customs-trader and customs-government administration interfaces should be influenced by international standards for information exchange. As a result, where all parties operate using the same standards, the software costs associated with electronic information exchange will also be drastically reduced.[193]

A significant challenge to be addressed when developing national single windows linked together to become a regional single window is the fact that the TFTA countries, though sharing a common ideal of deep integration do not share a common economic or developmental background.[194] The member countries of the TFTA find themselves today at different stages of development in all sectors including legal, socio-economic and political aspects of national development and still some lag behind in ICT connectivity more than their fellow regional counterparts.

In the same breathe, these disparities in development cannot be accepted as permanent inhibitors to the development of national single windows which are interconnected. While

---

[191] Duval Y, 'Legal Issues and Cross-Border Paperless Trade Facilitation' *ESCAP Work Programme on Electronic Single Window*, available at http://www.unescap.org/idd/events/2012-Colombo-meeting/6-1-Mr-Yann-D.pdf (accessed 18 April 2013).

[192] Kyoto Convention guidelines on the application of information and communication technology by the World Customs Organisation June 2004 at 52 available at http://www.insw.go.id/images/public/kyoto-ict-guidelines-wco.pdf (accessed 3 April 2013).

[193] Kyoto Convention guidelines on the application of information and communication technology by the World Customs Organisation June 2004 at 53 available at http://www.insw.go.id/images/public/kyoto-ict-guidelines-wco.pdf (accessed 3 April 2013).

[194] Thirlwall A and Hussain M, 'The Balance of payments constraint, capital flows and growth rate, differences between developing countries' *Oxford Economic Papers, New Series* (1982) 34, 498-510 at 500 available at http://down.cenet.org.cn/upfile/94/200512382736170.pdf (accessed 3 April 2013).

allowances should be given to allow each member state to develop a single window, there has to be a set time frame which is allocated to the countries. This is similar to the case of the Association of South East Asian Nations (ASEAN), which set out time frames for the development of the single window for its member countries.[195] This will ensure that all countries prioritise the program and mobilise resources and funding towards making the timeous implementation of the single window a reality.

Following on this frame of thought, it would be ideal and more efficient in the long term if the TFTA countries were to migrate to a common system for example the Automated System for Customs Data (ASYCUDA) world system. A significant number of the TFTA countries already have in place the ASYCUDA system and it would be strategic for all the countries in the regional economic community to adopt this system.[196] This electronic customs processing system can be modified as an interlinked single window and in addition to this, it is well supported by the United Nations Conference on Trade and Development (UNCTAD) and there is ample technical assistance to aid the TFTA member countries when setting up this system (those without ASYCUDA) or modifying it (for those already on ASYCUDA).[197] It has the further benefit that it is a system which has been tried and tested in addition to being verified as a reliable and safe platform for customs processing. ASYCUDA is also well recommended by the World Customs Organisation as a customs processing system.[198]

When implementing the single window system for the region on an ASYCUDA platform, it would be expedient and efficient for both the government and the trading community if any processing work which is done by an agency, such as document validation be easily accessible for viewing by other relevant agencies. This inter-linkage then acts as a safeguard against the duplication of information submitted and processed on the government ends and

---

[195] Experience on the Development of the ASEAN Single Window Negotiating Group on Trade Facilitation TN/TF/W/105 WTO Communication from ASEAN available at http://www.wcoomd.org/en/topics/facilitation/activities-and-programmes/wto-trade-facilitation-negotiations/~/media/131F8CBF311E4EDC92FFA774F64B2D28.ashx (accessed 4 April 2013).

[196] ASYCUDA in Africa information sheet AW-IS/MP/AF 25 available at http://www.unctadxi.org/sections/wsis/docs/asycuda/AW-IS-MP-AF-v4_en.pdf (accessed 3 April 2013); Zake J, 'Customs reform and Modernization in Anglophone Africa Early 1990s to mid 2010' *IMF working paper* WP11/184 available at http://www.imf.org/external/pubs/ft/wp/2011/wp11184.pdf (accessed 3 April 2013).

[197] UNCTAD Trust Fund for Trade Facilitation negotiations Technical Note No. 21 ASYCUDA available at http://unctad.org/en/docs/TN21_Asycuda.pdf (accessed 4 May 2013).

[198] David J, *ASYCUDA - A recommended IT system for a Customs-centric Single Window and Interconnectivity* UNCTAD Presentation at Casablanca, February 2013 available at http://www.itfc-idb.org/files/UNCTAD-ASYCUDA.pdf (accessed 3 April 2013).

duplication of effort on the industry (business) end.[199] Simultaneously, this interconnectivity will immediately create efficiencies for traders who only have to submit required information once with the reassurance that the same information will be disseminated to all the relevant agencies.

5.2.3 Obstacles to Design and Implementation

A factual challenge to the successful implementation of national single windows which are in turn regionally compatible with each other across the region is that of the continuation of political impetus and will among the leaders of the nations of the TFTA. While at the outset there may exist numerous commitments and pledges to the development of the project on paper, it may be a different scenario on the ground. It is not unusual that leaders are quick to pledge their commitment, but when it comes to the actual implementation, it immediately becomes a different conversation in terms of the actual implementation process.

At this point, the same leaders often times begin to back track on their initial commitments or drag their feet as they shift their focus to other programmes which may be more attractive to their domestic electorate in the short term. It must therefore be reiterated that as long as the political will wanes, the programme will plummet into the bottomless pit of marginalised regional programmes and be forgotten under a mountain of competing interests. If however, the leadership manages to overcome this challenge, the programme has significantly better odds of being a success and being implemented within the projected time frame.

One of the challenges which might also be faced by during the implementation of the single window programme might be the fact that some government agencies may have vested interests in polarising power and influence and therefore, through the introduction of a single window for the region, there would be devolution of power and decentralisation which would significantly reduce the power and influence of certain agencies.[200] These prospects of losing such power may then result in agencies or ministries displaying reluctance or to a certain extent, resistance to losing power and will try to guard their mandates closely in an effort to preserve procedure and artefacts of procedure.

---

[199] De Wulf L and Sokol J. B *Customs Modernization Handbook* (2005) 289.

[200] Hoekman B, Mattoo A, and English P (eds) *Development, Trade, and the WTO: A Handbook* (2002) 52.

However, despite these multiple potential challenges, once the preparatory process is successfully concluded and a lead agency[201] and its various working groups are established, the same preparatory process will have served as a building block towards promoting the sharing and development of common policies and strategies for sharing of information between relevant agencies especially customs administrations and continued evolution of the developed interoperable regional window.

The proposed implementation of the interconnected national single windows across the TFTA region would best be managed by the lead agency which should be charged with the coordination of the entire implementation project and also synchronises responsibilities between agencies in order to reduce a duplication of effort. The lead agency essentially refers to the government agency which may be appointed by member countries of the TFTA to coordinate, steer combined efforts by the various agencies involved and take the frontal role in the establishment and the implementation of the regional single window which is to be established.

5.3 COORDINATING EFFORTS BETWEEN AGENCIES

The lead agency will then coordinate efforts by all the national agencies and will be strategically poised such that it regularly oversees, monitors, coordinates, and reviews the implementation of the single windows, especially in light of compliance and conformity to the agreed format which the national single windows should take. The appropriate agency to lead the development of a single window may vary from country to country depending on the legal, political and organisational structure in each particular country. In most countries the lead agency will be the customs administration.[202] In addition, an over-arching lead agency in charge of the entire process will further allow for the easier identification and modification of processes to increase efficiencies.

In this regard, when each member state develops its national single window, it must be kept in mind that the model should meet internationally acceptable standards.[203] In order to

[201] McLinden G et al. *Border Management Modernization* (2011) 17-9.
[202] McLinden G et al, *Border Management Modernization* (2011) 100.
[203] ECONOMIC COMMISSION FOR EUROPE United Nations Centre for Trade Facilitation and Electronic Business (UN/CEFACT) recommendation 33. Recommendation and Guidelines on establishing a Single Window to

achieve these outcomes, the lead agency should ideally therefore be one which possesses the necessary authority and political support essential to successfully carry through the vision of implementing the single window. The lead agency should then be charged with assembling a high powered project management group to drive the programme.

Once responsibilities have been defined, the lead agency should then be charged with the duty of assembling various working parties to focus on specific aspects of the development of the single windows. This is due to the fact that the process of harmonisation of the ICT and legal aspects of customs will also require that there be a comprehensive overhaul of the status quo and as a result this project will demand input and expertise from various agencies and ministries.[204] The working parties will therefore ideally be made up of representatives from the said agencies and ministries involved.

Each working party will be assigned to fulfilling specific tasks with a unique focus on specific aspects at each stage of the harmonisation process. These work groups should ideally be composed of highly qualified experts in the relevant areas to be developed.[205] In addition, it will be imperative to the success of the project that there should be information sharing between the work groups as well as the identification of areas for collaboration between the work groups.

In addition, in the implementation of the interconnected national single windows, the establishment of an overarching process flow document will have to be drafted which will set out a broadly outline of all the key processes to be followed.[206] Once there is set in place a clear process flow or thought process for the project, there will be an increased and more productive collaboration between the different agencies involved and affords a better demarcation and understanding of specific roles within the entire process and the resultant inter linkages.

---

enhance the efficient exchange of information between trade and government *http://www.unece.org/fileadmin/DAM/cefact/recommendations/rec33/rec33_trd352e.pdf* (accessed 3 April 2013).

[204] Towards a single window trading environment: Achieving effective stakeholder coordination United Nations Network of Experts for paperless trade in Asia and the Pacific Brief no.7 September 2011 available at *http://www.unescap.org/unnext/pub/brief7.pdf* (accessed 3 April 2013).

[205] McLinden G et al, *Border Management Modernization* (2011) 15.

[206] Key Factors in Establishing Single Windows for Handling Import/Export Procedures and Formalities: Trade Facilitation and the Single Window E/ESCWA/EDGD/2011/5 10 November 2011 at 27 available at *http://www.wto.org/english/tratop_e/tradfa_e/case_studies_e/escwa_e.pdf* (accessed 3 April 2013).

A fundamental requirement which is essential to the success of the harmonisation programme is that the lead organisation which should be charged with steering and coordinating the process and the various work groups involved in the harmonisation of ICT and customs legislation should ensure that there is actual simplification and harmonisation and not merely the creation of another lateral layer of legislation and procedure. The harmonisation programme will essentially adopt a top down approach which cannot be driven without acceptance from agency or ministry heads. In short therefore, the leading or coordinating agency should possess the necessary authority to define and coordinate implementation, operations, and resource management.[207]

In addition, this lead agency will also have the singular task of reviewing the implementation of the agreement and provide support to the various agencies and the ministries involved in the development of the single windows. There is in addition, a need to also develop a shared services environment during the development and implementation phases of the TFTA regional single window.[208] This is an important consideration which cannot be overlooked without suffering dire consequences. Within a regional framework, the shared services environment greatly assists in the avoidance of duplication of efforts by working parties and simultaneously increases efficiencies, developmental milestones are achieved more rapidly and the financial overheads are significantly reduced.

The shared services approach however would require consensus to be reached by the participating countries in terms of the design or construction pattern which the sharing model or framework would take. This would also require a further agreement on the common basic procedures to be followed and how progress, delays and unforeseen events are to be reported. By adopting a shared services approach, the participating agencies and the various working groups would then be in a better position to rapidly attain the regional harmonisation of ICT and legislation of customs for the region while allowing the lead agency to drive and coordinate the process.[209]

---

[207] Towards a single window trading environment: Achieving effective stakeholder coordination United Nations Network of Experts for paperless trade in Asia and the Pacific Brief no.7 September 2011 available at *http://www.unescap.org/unnext/pub/brief7.pdf* (accessed 3 April 2013).

[208] McLinden G et al, *Border Management Modernization* (2011) 16.

[209] McLinden G et al, *Border Management Modernization* (2011) 16.

A further challenge which is quite often the most obvious hamper to fulfilling any project is that of financing. The TFTA as reiterated before is made up of economies which are at different stages of development and most are cash strapped and have multiple pressing needs which all are to be serviced on a budget which constrained and has multiple competing interests. This financing challenge could be addressed through engaging the private sector across the TFTA region and courting suitable partners for a private-public- partnership with the governments of the TFTA.

In terms of this private-public-partnership arrangement, the private sector would be more involved to the benefit of all border management agencies using the available services.[210] For example, a shared document management function could reduce the rate of growth of documentation stored at each fragmented individual agency. While a private-public-partnership arrangement would be a feasible financing option, a governance structure would nevertheless be needed to direct and monitor performance.

Another financing alternative would be for each border management agency to source and secure political and financial commitment to tailor the collaborative border management concept to its own requirements, assess its administrative capacity, develop its transformation program, select the right partners to support the program, and evolve and align its business models and technical strategies in ways that demonstrate the value of collaborative border management to both governments and citizens. [211]

5.4 CREATING A REGIONAL LEGAL FRAMEWORK FOR THE SINGLE WINDOW

Once a ICT framework has been established around the form that the single window should take for the TFTA region, the next step will be that of developing a regional legal framework which will govern the single window, set out the rights and obligations of the various governments and their relevant agencies towards each other in terms of the sharing, privacy,

---

[210] Towards a single window trading environment: Achieving effective stakeholder coordination United Nations Network of Experts for paperless trade in Asia and the Pacific Brief no.7 September 2011 available at *http://www.unescap.org/unnext/pub/brief7.pdf* (accessed 3 April 2013).

[211] Key Factors in Establishing Single Windows for Handling Import/Export Procedures and Formalities: Trade Facilitation and the Single Window E/ESCWA/EDGD/2011/5 10 November 2011 at 27 available at *http://www.wto.org/english/tratop_e/tradfa_e/case_studies_e/escwa_e.pdf* (accessed 3 April 2013).

and conservation of information.[212] The legal framework will also have to take into account the need to also regulate the process of harmonisation of information by all the national agencies and set up a framework for a sustainable system of information exchange.

The development of the regional legal framework will then guide and inform the corresponding national legislation to be developed in each of the TFTA member states which will flesh out the regional framework. In addition, the legal framework will have to take into consideration a number of pertinent issues including the fact that when designing the electronic single window for the region the legal issues to be taken into consideration should include the following key concerns:[213]

i) Security considerations such as the format in which data will take when being stored, authentication of documents and signatures, and information disseminated on the system.[214]
ii) Confidentiality concerns which may include the restrictions on data sharing and accessibility thereof between governments and relevant agencies utilising the regional single window,[215]
iii) Other general overarching issues which encompass evidentiary issues, rights and obligations, provisions which address residual uses of manual documentation and how the system will be launched and when.

The above considerations form an integral significant part of this discussion and will be specifically addressed below, and according a specific focus on formulating the most favourable approach towards adopting a regional protocol for the TFTA. The discussion will also address the need to develop not just a single window facility for the region but also

---

[212] Luddy W *ASEAN Single window: The intersection of law and technology* Paper presented to ASEAN Secretariat (2008) 17 available at http://pdf.usaid.gov/pdf_docs/PNADM816.pdf accessed 3 April 2013).
[213] Kyoto Convention guidelines on the application of information and communication technology by the World Customs Organisation June 2004 available at http://www.insw.go.id/images/public/kyoto-ict-guidelines-wco.pdf (accessed 3 April 2013).
[214] Luddy W. 'Single Window and Paperless Trade Legal Issues: A Possible Mosaic' Global Trade Facilitation Conference 2011 available at http://www.unece.org/fileadmin/DAM/trade/Trade_Facilitation_Forum/ConferencePPTs/D02_08AM_BillLuddy.pdf. (accessed 4 April 2013).
[215] Puggliatti L, 'Cloud single window: legal implications of a new model of cross-border single window' (2011) 5 *WCJ* 13 available at http://www.worldcustomsjournal.org/media/wcj/-2011/2/Pugliatti.pdf (accessed 4 May 2013).

develop a system which complies with international standards which is truly integrated or harmonised.

5.4.1 Adopting a regional protocol for the regulation of the single window.

The proposed legal framework would ideally be adopted in the form of a customs protocol, which protocol would then form the basis upon which, the member states may draft their corresponding legislation in order to align it with the said protocol. Once this is agreed upon by the members states of the TFTA then the same regional protocol will have to be drafted in such a manner that it is aligned to internationally accepted standards set and incorporates enough flexibility to allow national legislations to draft their domestic laws according to the blueprint without compromising on their need to customise the law to their various stages of development and bespoke country specifications.[216]

It is imperative that the regional customs protocol also ensure that issues related to the admissibility of electronically generated information are addressed especially in light of the fact that the WCO, has repeatedly advocated for its members to pass legislation to this effect and also make provision for the authentication of computer readable data by means other than handwritten signature. These are essential legal reforms not only from a customs viewpoint but also from the viewpoint of the trading community as well.[217]

The harmonisation of customs legislation and regulations among the TFTA member countries and the corresponding simplification and standardisation of procedures and full computerisation of all processes are all key elements of the characteristics of the proposed customs protocol. These measures have a particular significance for the subsequent further integration of the national single window systems not only as a means of protecting and increasing customs revenues but also of providing secure facilitation of the movement of goods into and out of the region.

---

[216] Puggliatti L, 'Cloud single window: legal implications of a new model of cross-border single window' (2011) 5 *WCJ* 13 available at http://www.worldcustomsjournal.org/media/wcj/-2011/2/Pugliatti.pdf (accessed 4 May 2013).

[217] Kyoto Convention guidelines on the application of information and communication technology by the World Customs Organisation June 2004 at 82 available at http://www.insw.go.id/images/public/kyoto-ict-guidelines-wco.pdf (accessed 3 April 2013); Luddy W *ASEAN Single window: The intersection of law and technology* Paper presented to ASEAN Secretariat (2008) 17 available at http://pdf.usaid.gov/pdf_docs/PNADM816.pdf accessed 3 April 2013).

In addition, it would be preferable if the customs protocol were to make specific provisions for the design of the national single windows especially when considering the need to ensure that there is an emphasis on the reduction of costs of trade. This said reduction should further be identified and elaborated as emanating from the simplification and harmonisation of customs procedures through customs cooperation of the various TFTA customs administrations. It should also incorporate recommended international best practices and customs procedures to the greatest extent possible.

Developing a harmonised ICT system and in addition developing a regional customs protocol which initiates the harmonisation of the national laws pertaining to customs in the TFTA region is a complex task requiring the balanced interplay between various players within the government and the private sector. While it may be onerous and almost impossible to be compliant with all the relevant laws within a manual customs processing environment, it is quite the opposite within a well designed electronic processing environment.[218]

This is due the fact that the electronic system would have been designed and developed in such a manner that it is aligned to the legal requirements and hence should there be any amendments or developments to the legal framework, the processing system can also be accordingly updated to immediately reflect the change in the status quo. In addition, customs could also make use of international data standards in order to achieve a uniform system across the TFTA region to ensure that whenever laws are changed the system is adapted accordingly.

5.4.2 Developing an internationally accepted customs processing system

As previously discussed in chapter two, a single automated electronic customs system will vastly change the trading environment for TFTA countries and their industries creating a paradigm shift in overall business methodology. The implementation of a single automated electronic customs system will have to work within an enabling environment where domestic

[218] Kyoto Convention guidelines on the application of information and communication technology by the World Customs Organisation June 2004 at 13 available at http://www.insw.go.id/images/public/kyoto-ict-guidelines-wco.pdf (accessed 3 April 2013).

customs legislation has been aligned and is similar across the entire TFTA region[219] else the electronic single window project would be a matter of placing the cart before the horse. This is because of the fact that for as long as disparities exist in national policies and legal frameworks, the regional single window implementation project may well become a white elephant which will fail to produce the desired and anticipated joint economic gains.

When harmonising the current pieces of national legislation of the TFTA member countries in place, firstly a total review of the domestic laws in the various domestic jurisdictions must be undertaken.[220] The domestic legislation relating to the various customs laws should then be uniformly aligned and developed in order to enable the streamlining of national legislation in line with the recommendations of the Revised Kyoto Convention and the developed regional customs protocol. The customs administrations will also need to make decisions during the design of the legal and ICT frameworks in respect of the parameters relating to which processes should remain at a national level or could perhaps be open to regulation at the regional level.

In this regard, there should be developed a general framework as an annex to the customs protocol bearing with certain specific guidelines which will allow domestic legislation to adopt without necessarily rescinding sovereignty. The annex could even take the form of a draft model legislation which the member states may follow closely or modify as necessary.

This draft model of domestic legislation may be an acceptable compromise considering the fact that most states will be reluctant to give up the flexibility of their sovereignty and would not be happy to be forced into a situation whereby they are obliged to adopt a singular legislation. Through the adoption of a draft legislative framework which sets out what is to be included within domestic legislation, the member states will not feel that their sovereignty is compromised as they can additionally address other domestic matters within their own modified legislation whilst simultaneously ensuring that such legislation remains aligned to the letter of the regional customs protocol and guidelines.

---

[219] Zake J, 'Customs reform and Modernization in Anglophone Africa Early 1990s to mid 2010' *IMF working paper* WP11/184 available at *http://www.imf.org/external/pubs/ft/wp/2011/wp11184.pdf* (accessed 3 April 2013).

[220] Luddy W. 'Single Window and Paperless Trade Legal Issues: A Possible Mosaic' Global Trade Facilitation Conference 2011 available at *http://www.unece.org/fileadmin/DAM/trade/Trade_Facilitation_Forum/ConferencePPTs/D02_08AM_BillLuddy.pdf*. (accessed 4 April 2013).

In addition, there should also be established a monitoring body over the implementation of the regional legislative framework for the ICT customs system which is to be adopted in the various member countries.[221] This monitoring mechanism will allow for a regular review and analysis of the efforts by the member states in developing national legal and regulatory frameworks that will govern the functions and operations of the electronic national service window and will be a critical area in concordance with the regional customs protocol.

The customs protocol should clearly define the legal basis upon which electronic transactions will be processed and accepted, it should also address the issues surrounding the legal admissibility of these transactions, and the legal ability and the *locus standi* of relevant agencies to accept and process electronic transactions.[222] All these matters should be clearly defined before the single windows are interconnected and running. A key aspect previously identified in the drafting of the protocol is that of data sharing. This will have to be detailed clearly with regards to the information to be shared and not shared and in this regard, the parties authorised to access the information should be identified. The information sharing parameters could also be further integrated into national legislation.[223]

The relevant legal analysis preceding the drafting of the customs protocol should then focus on identifying disparities, gaps and impediments in national laws, as well as existent regulations which may possibly hamper the successful implementation of the interconnected national single windows across the TFTA region.[224] In this respect, cooperation by TFTA member states with respect to developing similar domestic policies on the trade enabling environment can substantially increase the economic gains from forming such a regional economic community. Policy integration for the members of the TFTA can lift invisible

---

[221] Zake J, 'Customs reform and Modernization in Anglophone Africa Early 1990s to mid 2010' *IMF working paper* WP11/184 available at http://www.imf.org/external/pubs/ft/wp/2011/wp11184.pdf (accessed 3 April 2013).

[222] Key Factors in Establishing Single Windows for Handling Import/Export Procedures and Formalities: Trade Facilitation and the Single Window E/ESCWA/EDGD/2011/5 10 November 2011 at 27 available at http://www.wto.org/english/tratop_e/tradfa_e/case_studies_e/escwa_e.pdf (accessed 3 April 2013).

[223] Luddy W. 'Single Window and Paperless Trade Legal Issues: A Possible Mosaic' Global Trade Facilitation Conference 2011 available at http://www.unece.org/fileadmin/DAM/trade/Trade_Facilitation_Forum/ConferencePPTs/D02_08AM_BillLuddy.pdf. (accessed 4 April 2013).

[224] Messerlin P, Zarouk J, 'Trade Facilitation: Technical regulations and customs procedures', *World Economy* 23, (2000) Vol. 4 584-587.

barriers which insulate national markets from economic advantages.[225] In the same breathe; cooperation on domestic policies can also act as safeguards against member states which may unscrupulously consider reverting back to imposing trade protectionist trade restrictions through the back door.

Intergovernmental cooperation will also be essential in the formulation and resultant application of domestic policies which will include broader areas to improve trade facilitation including such areas as taxes, enforcement of sanitary and phyto-sanitary measures, health and safety regulations, environmental standards.[226] Once these policies are successfully implemented in the presence of an efficient single window for the entire TFTA region, these combined successes could well act as compelling stimuli of foreign direct investment into a region which has a uniform customs processing system and correspondingly clear legislation.[227]

Additionally, from a regional perspective, the successful launching of a single window for customs across the TFTA could also have the positive spin-off effect of increasing intra-regional competition through the reduction of transaction costs which allows new suppliers to enter the regional market more easily and true comparative advantage begins to manifest among producers in the region.

5.5 <u>POST IMPLEMENTATION CHALLENGES</u>

Customs administrations have the unfortunate reputation of being generally regarded as corruption riddled organisations.[228] This negative perception by the industry and private

---

[225] Key Factors in Establishing Single Windows for Handling Import/Export Procedures and Formalities: Trade Facilitation and the Single Window E/ESCWA/EDGD/2011/5 10 November 2011 at 18 available at *http://www.wto.org/english/tratop_e/tradfa_e/case_studies_e/escwa_e.pdf* (accessed 3 April 2013); Schiff M and Winters A. L, *Regional integration and development* (2003) 147.

[226] Koh Tat Tsen. J (2011) available at *http://www.unece.org/fileadmin/DAM/trade/Trade_Facilitation_Forum/BkgrdDocs/TenYearsSingleWindow.pdf* (accessed 4 May 2013).

[227] Luddy W. 'Single Window and Paperless Trade Legal Issues: A Possible Mosaic' Global Trade Facilitation Conference 2011 available at *http://www.unece.org/fileadmin/DAM/trade/Trade_Facilitation_Forum/ConferencePPTs/D02_08AM_BillLuddy.pdf*. (accessed 4 April 2013).

[228] Key Factors in Establishing Single Windows for Handling Import/Export Procedures and Formalities: Trade Facilitation and the Single Window E/ESCWA/EDGD/2011/5 10 November 2011 at 19 available at *http://www.wto.org/english/tratop_e/tradfa_e/case_studies_e/escwa_e.pdf* (accessed 3 April 2013).

sector may become an inhibiting factor when government tries to introduce the concept of a single window in a bid to bring the private sector involved especially when seeking to embark on private-public-partnership development arrangements. In order to counteract this negative perception, the TFTA would have to conduct national workshops in each of the member countries where the private sector is invited to information sharing sessions and educated about the benefits of the single window and also highlights that with the advent of an regional single window, fraudulent behaviour will become more difficult to mask.

Another challenge that may exist is that of the concurrent existence of a manual processing system together with the new regional window that would have been developed. This delay in phasing out the manual system before fully migrating to the electronic system slow down a customs administration and as such any efficiency to be gained may not be apparent. It is to be emphasised that although ICT is not the panacea to the effectiveness of a customs administration, it does contribute significantly towards lowering the costs of trade.[229]

ICT implementation is closely linked with the increase in efficiencies within the work environment. This however does not mean that implementation of a single window will immediately translate into miraculous efficiencies. The single window should be recognised as a tool for change and not the actual change. Therefore, the electronic processing system will have to be used by an administration which is well trained otherwise the envisaged efficiencies will not be realised.[230]

Customs reform demands an ongoing awareness of the developments which take place in international trade. Therefore, in light of this, the implementation of the regional single window and the corresponding drafting of accompanying legislation to regulate the anticipated relationship between the various users of the single window will not be an event but will rather be a process. In addition, what is developed will not be cast into stone but there should be a continued analysis of the systems put into place and incrementally develop it in line with the changes and developments in international trade.

---

[229] Zake J, 'Customs reform and Modernization in Anglophone Africa Early 1990s to mid 2010' *IMF working paper* WP11/184 available at *http://www.imf.org/external/pubs/ft/wp/2011/wp11184.pdf* (accessed 3 April 2013).

[230] Kyoto Convention guidelines on the application of information and communication technology by the World Customs Organisation June 2004 at 16 available at *http://www.insw.go.id/images/public/kyoto-ict-guidelines-wco.pdf* (accessed 3 April 2013).

While it may not be a problem identifying a single window system to implement, the obstacle to implementation may appear in the form of lack of local technical expertise. In this regard, before the system is fully implemented in the member countries of the TFTA, the staff who will make use of the single window system should be adequately trained and educated about the system and how it works in order for the transition from manual operation to electronic operation be smoother and faster. The staff should also be made aware of the fact that the two modes of operation cannot co-exist *ad infinitum* and accordingly the manual mode should be used less and only in instances where the electronic system has not yet been fully developed to cater or address a particular requirement.

Another noteworthy challenge to be faced when implementing a regional single window will be that of managing potential legal liability.[231] In terms of this potentially debilitating hurdle which may open up a vast number of claims, It will be essential that there be developed end-user agreements to be signed by traders who will interact with the customs administrations using the anticipated single windows. It would be advisable that the prototype of the agreement include demarcations as to the extent and limitation of liability in any transaction. Further to this, it would be prudent to include alternative dispute resolution options such as arbitration or mediation in the event of a dispute arising between parties.

Inasmuch as these risks are addressed, it should be noted that the potential for legal liability might still arise in several other contexts in the operation of the single window. Liability could extend to instances such as data processing errors or breaches which may have negative financial implications. These operational hazards are further compounded in a regional setting as the single window will be operational across national borders. This may well result in scenarios where foreign litigants seeking redress for damages may need to approach national courts in the TFTA region resulting in an escalation of claims against customs administrations in the region.[232]

---

[231] Recommendation 35 – *Establishing a legal framework for international trade Single Window*, October 2010, UNCEFACT (2010) available at www.unece.org/cefact/recommendations/rec35/Rec35-PublicReviewDraftv9-Feb09.doc (accessed 3 April 2013).

[232] Luddy W. 'Single Window and Paperless Trade Legal Issues: A Possible Mosaic' Global Trade Facilitation Conference 2011 available at http://www.unece.org/fileadmin/DAM/trade/Trade_Facilitation_Forum/ConferencePPTs/D02_08AM_BillLuddy.pdf. (accessed 4 April 2013).

5.6 CONCLUSION

From the above discussion, it becomes clear that the proposal of a regional single window customs system for the TFTA region is one which will demand a clear thought process commencing from the point of conceptualisation through to the actual design and eventual implementation. The proposed harmonisation and simplification of customs laws is therefore one side of the coin, with the ICT single window comprising the other side of the same coin. Any reforms designed at reforming the customs processing system for the region will of necessity demand an accompanying reform of legislation to support the successful implementation of the said regional single window system.

At every stage of the process, it is imperative that all the proposed actors are involved and fully informed. This includes the governments of the TFTA who will have to stamp their approval on the initial blueprint of the idea and also need to carry through the vision of the single window to their various relevant country agencies. The legislative framework, in the form of the regional protocol on customs and its related domestic legislations, which is then eventually adopted should also reflect within it transit related provisions and leverage technology and security requirements.

If a satisfactory equilibrium is then struck, the successful progression of the project will begin to manifest through incremental achievement of the desired outcomes which have been discussed previously in this mini-thesis, which are essentially the reduction of the costs of trade deriving from harmonised, simpler and clearer customs procedures. Through this collective regional achievement, the TFTA will be poised to assume its position within the international trade arena, to actively participate therein as a powerful economic force, no longer from the peripherals but deep within the hub of economic activity, directing the path of African growth through effective regional integration and ensuring that foreign direct investment growth is sustained and improved upon as investors are lured into a lucrative economic region which is attractive due to its high ease of conducting legitimate business.

CHAPTER 6: SUMMARY OF FINDINGS AND CONCLUSION

6.1 FINDINGS

This mini-thesis has sought to address a number of questions which pertain to the harmonisation of customs policies and legislation across the Tripartite Free Trade Agreement (TFTA) area with a view to achieving deeper integration and economic growth for its member countries collectively. While it is recognised that the TFTA is still a work in progress, it is forward thinking for any regional economic community to envision future developments and the evolution in its lifecycle from one stage to the next in terms of deeper integration efforts.[233]

For any progressive regional economic community, when conceptualising the ideal form of regional integration vehicle to employ, it should be acknowledged that it is generally more complicated to create a Customs Union (CU) as opposed to creating a Free Trade Area (FTA).[234] While it can be more demanding from the perspective that the creation and development of a CU requires intensive and ongoing coordination, it is economically more lucrative than an FTA in that it poses the benefit of deeper market integration.[235]

Thus said, the focal point of the thesis has been upon the reduction of exorbitant costs of trade which are currently characteristic of the TFTA member countries, as part of greater measures towards increasing collective efforts in trade facilitation. In this sense, customs is a major area of international trade which was addressed as a relevant sector for regulatory and technological reform through the harmonisation of legislation across the region and the development of a single customs processing system to compliment and enable collective legislative efforts by the members of the TFTA.[236]

The second chapter introduced the single window as a system and as a user experience to the discussion. It brought to the fore the relevance of a single window for the region whilst exploring the different features and advantages of the single window customs processing

---

[233] See chapter 3 at paragraph 3.3.
[234] See discussion at page 17.
[235] Hoekman B, et al (eds) *Development, Trade, and the WTO: A Handbook* (2002) 548.
[236] See chapter 3 paragraph 3.1.

system.[237] In the process of identifying the capabilities of the single window customs processing system, the variant forms which a single window system can adopt were also discussed and the features of each different model of the single window were correspondingly identified.

The benefits of adopting a single window customs processing system for the TFTA and the benefits of modernising a customs administration in order to remain competitive or to gain a competitive advantage in the arena of global trade were also succinctly set out in the second chapter.[238] Once the single window was identified and its benefits and disadvantages analysed, it became necessary to carry out an assessment of the current efforts which the fledgling TFTA has made so far in a bid to reduce the costs of trade and increase trade facilitation efforts.

From the findings, it appears that the TFTA is a grouping which does indeed aim towards deeper integration[239] but currently the efforts being undertaken are disparate due to the fact that at the implementation level, there are various stakeholders exerting parallel efforts at the individual Regional Economic Community (REC) level to the extent that some programmes could be merged across the three REC's comprising the TFTA in order to reduce the duplication of efforts and to streamline costs. From this examination of current customs harmonisation efforts by the TFTA the thesis shifted to a specific examination of the European Union (EU) as a customs union (CU)[240].

As part of the themes explored in this thesis, there has also been an analysis of the customs union of the EU through the tracing of its development and successes. The EU was specifically chosen for analysis as it is a functional and efficient CU besides taking into account its other successful facets. In this regard, chapter four focused on the EU as an advanced regional economic community and model from which the TFTA could learn from in terms of establishing a successful customs union with an efficient customs processing

---

[237] As discussed in detail at chapter 2 paragraph 2.2.

[238] See chapter 2 at paragraph 2.3 which motivates the adoption and development of a regional single window.

[239] Hartzenberg T 'Regional Integration in Africa' *Staff Working Paper ERSD*-2011-14, WTO Economic Research and Statistics Division (2011). Available at http://www.wto.org/english/res_e/reser_e/ersd201114_e.pdf (accessed 25 April 2013).

[240] See chapter 4 at paragraph 4.1.

system. In this regard, the EU was the most appropriate REC to analyse due to the fact that it is a well-established REC.

From the analysis it was also observed that the EU has managed to harmonise its customs laws through the introduction of a modernised customs code which is effectively a supranational document that directs customs activities for all member states in the EU. The EU today is now in actual fact more than just a mere grouping of countries but has now attained the form of a supranational body which has far reaching authority so much that the grouping even has a functional parliament which rivals the national parliaments of the member states in terms of authority.[241]

The modernised customs code has been a success to date; and in terms of the technological aspects of the single customs processing system, the challenge which remains for the EU is that of transforming and adapting successful established national single window systems into one regional interconnected system.[242] The EU vision is that of developing a fully interoperable customs processing system which encompasses all relevant regulatory authorities in order to satisfy trader compliance with customs regulatory requirements. It should be added that the EU is at advanced stages of actualising this vision.

In the aforementioned analysis, it became clear that the single window customs processing system could be successfully adapted to suit the needs of the TFTA in order to generate significant economic benefits for the TFTA. After identifying the single window and what it holds in store for the TFTA and further assessing its benefits in terms of other successful REC's, it became necessary to propose the adoption of a regional single window for the TFTA. This proposal came with the corresponding need which was identified of developing a legal framework for the TFTA region which would be focused on customs and the single window.[243] It was further identified that the development of a single window for customs is to be implemented in sync together with the harmonisation of customs legislation across the entire region as the two projects could well be equated to being two faces of a single coin.

---

[241] See as discussed in chapter 4 at paragraphs 4.4 and 4.5.

[242] European Commission: Taxation and Customs Union-Electronic_customs_initiative It_projects available at http://ec.europa.eu/taxation_customs/customs/policy_issues/electronic_customs_initiative/it_projects/ (last accessed 21 April 2013).

[243] See chapter 5, discussed paragraph 5.4.

A good regional customs protocol for the TFTA in the area of customs will be able to define the parameters of cooperation for an enabling national legislative framework which includes the following characteristics discussed further.[244] The legislative framework should be able to set out clearly the competences of customs and make adequate provision for compliance with international commitments such as World Trade Organisation (WTO) agreements. To add to this requisite characteristic, the national legislative frameworks should also be easily accessible, transparent and predictable through the provision of basic information regarding rules, procedures and penalties for non-compliance.[245]

From the identification of the single window as a trade facilitation tool to aid in the processing of customs, chapter five embarks on a journey where the single window is targeted as a suitable system to be adopted by the TFTA. In doing so it is acknowledged that the single window system has to be developed according to the specifications of the region as it cannot be transposed from one system due to the unique challenges and bespoke requirements of each regional grouping.[246]

From the discussions in the previous chapters, it was also clarified that a single window customs processing system will only be successfully implemented within an enabling environment where there are high levels of government and political commitment, and the private sector is well advised and involved at every phase of the process. This involvement of all parties will allow ownership of the single window and its eventual evolution by all the stakeholders with anticipated ongoing regional economic development and cooperation.

6.2 RECOMMENDATIONS

When drafting and formulating the regional protocol for customs which has been proposed in this thesis, the protocol should ideally, address the framework of cooperation and points of reference between the private sector, national customs administrations and related

[244] See discussion in chapter 5 at 5.4.2.

[245] Prechal S. & De Leeuw E, *'General Principles of EC Law in A Process of Development: Reports from A Conference in Stockholm'* 202. Available at *http://www.uu.nl/faculty/leg/NL/organisatie/departementen/departementrechtsgeleerdheid/organisatie/onderdelen/europainstituut/publicaties/algemenerechtsbeginselen/Documents/S.%20Prechal%20en%20M.E.%20de%20Leeuw,%20Transparancy.pdf* (accessed 25 April 2013).

[246] See discussion in chapter 5 at 5.4.2.

governmental agencies within the region while ensuring continued adherence to international standards.

The Revised Kyoto Convention (RKC) is an international instrument which could prove to be indispensible in the drafting of the protocol as it was developed to assist countries in their attempts to harmonise customs policies and procedures. Through the use of the RKC as a basic point of reference and departure,[247] the TFTA could draft a design of customs processes which is in compliance with international conventions and obligations, a specific case in point being Articles V, VIII and X of the General Agreement on Tariffs and Trade (GATT) 1994.

The regional customs protocol to be drafted could also be viewed as an effective step in regional integration efforts. This viewpoint stems from the fact that regional integration can take many forms and can occur at various levels[248] of cooperation between countries; it can also encompass a vast array of sectors or areas. In terms of cooperation between countries in the realm of legislative and policy integration, there is often a certain measure of resistance or reluctance which may be encountered towards the merging of policies or the creation of uniform legal frameworks in certain areas especially as African countries often guard the concept of sovereignty closely.

Additionally, as an area within the theory of regional integration, the concept of legislative and policy cooperation can also be used as an aid in setting up a supervisory institution specifically to monitor compliance with the adopted customs protocol. To compound to this theory, the idea of legislative harmonisation as a tool for regional integration in the area of customs cooperation may at first have appeared unpalatable but it has been elucidated and motivated in this thesis[249] that the relative loss of sovereignty which accompanies this level of commitment and structure of regional integration can actually produce positive economic spin-offs which benefit the members of the TFTA.

---

[247] De Wulf .L and Sokol J.B *Customs Modernization Handbook* (2005) 57.

[248] Schiff M and Winters A. L, *Regional integration and development* (2003) 2; 189.

[249] As discussed at page 61.

According to De Wulf and Sokol[250], outdated customs legislation has the negative effect of constraining social and economic progress by acting as significant non-tariff trade barriers. Such obsolete legislation prevents the effective collection of revenue, discourages foreign trade and investment, and potentially threatens social and national security. This view therefore promotes new laws for customs which are progressive and dynamic in tune with global trends in trade. For the TFTA this would translate into the adoption of a progressive looking customs protocol aimed at streamlining customs across the region.

In reaching a decision on the structure which the overarching protocol and the national legislation will take, it may be more efficient for the member countries to design the legislation to be adopted in the form of a code. A single customs code promises a number of benefits in comparison to drafting separate pieces of legislation. The most obvious advantage which a code has over multiple pieces of legislation is that it will be significantly easier for a trader to research and obtain information on applicable rules and regulations within a single consolidated code than in multiple pieces of legislation. A code is also easier to amend than multiple laws because any amendments are simply incorporated into the code without creating opportunities for conflict with other customs related legislation.[251]

From the previous chapters, it also is evident that the focal point of regional integration should also be on the promotion of free intra-regional trade and the antecedent removal of non-tariff barriers across the TFTA which could be achieved effectively through the implementation of a single customs processing system. In this regard, while it is to be remembered that it is essential for a single window system be developed and implemented regionally as part of a greater effort towards reducing the costs of trade through the accompanying reduction of non-tariff barriers, there also exists simultaneously and in parallel, the critical need to facilitate and create opportunities for the injection of foreign direct investment into the regional economy. This could be achieved as elucidated above, through the attraction of investors with a streamlined, harmonised and efficient customs processing system which is transparent and bulwarked by uniform national legislative frameworks which are grounded in an authoritative regional protocol.

---

[250] De Wulf .L and Sokol J.B *Customs Modernization Handbook* (2005) 52.

[251] See discussion in chapter 5 at 5.4.

6.3 CONCLUSION

It is inevitable that customs laws and processing systems across the TFTA region will have to undergo a thorough process of customs modernisation and streamlining if the region is to attract foreign direct investment to complement intra-regional trade successes. This is due to the fact that while intra-regional trade will definitely increase with deeper integration, it unfortunately has limits in its potential to drive economic growth. Foreign direct investment is an accepted tool for economic growth especially for small fragmented states with equally small economies which are often heavily reliant on a single sector which contributes to a major proportion of the GDP.[252]

While this thesis has identified the need to create a harmonised system for customs processing and a unified legislative framework to bolster the technological framework which would have been implemented, there are also ever present challenges which have to be addressed and managed accordingly. These challenges are coupled together with sacrifices to be made by all parties involved. Such sacrifices to be made include the giving up of sovereignty on a relative level stemming from the creation of national domestic legislation which corresponds to a regional customs protocol for the TFTA. On the other hand, the idea of national legislation being informed by a regional protocol could be more positively viewed as a 'pooling of sovereignty.'

Every country and every regional economic community (REC) is unique. Depending on unique regional priorities and readiness of the member states, the design of a single window will depend on region-specific requirements. Despite all these hampering factors, the successful implementation of a single window will yield marked improvements in overall trade facilitation indicators.[253] In the same breath, the results of implementing a single window customs processing system and its accompanying harmonised legislation may not be immediately evident in the short term, but as aforesaid in the previous chapters, in the presence of a sturdy and certain legislative framework; investors are more inclined to

[252] Hartzenberg T 'Regional Integration in Africa' *Staff Working Paper ERSD*-2011-14, WTO Economic Research and Statistics Division (2011) available at http://www.wto.org/english/res_e/reser_e/ersd201114_e.pdf (accessed 25 April 2013).

[253] Koh Tat Tsen J 'Single Windows in developing countries: Sharing experiences and lessons learnt from countries in the region and region initiatives' ESCAP-ECO Joint Trade Facilitation Forum on paperless trade and single window, 25-25 May (2012) available at http://www.unescap.org/tid/projects/swiran-s6koh.pdf (accessed 18 April 2013).

establish business operations in the TFTA region due to a positive investment climate. As a result thereof, the economic gains will then begin to manifest in various ways across the economy.

The development of a system which allows for paperless trade in customs introduces the seamless or uniform recognition of documents through the standardisation of requirements and ease of input and uniform compliance requirements by national authorities across the TFTA economic region. This idea of a paperless customs processing environment has also been closely linked with the concept of integrated border management for customs which has often been applied within a national context but could be broadened to regional application as a trade facilitation concept aimed at increasing the operating efficiency of customs agencies.

The TFTA is now in the process of designing a uniform or harmonised single administrative customs document for the three REC's in addition to this, it also recently embarked upon a project to standardise customs cooperation provisions for information exchange pertaining to customs legislation modifications, procedures and duties, including the exchange of information on regulatory requirements. In essence, member state customs systems and practices should be convergent, and the automated customs systems have to be fully interoperable in order to enable the seamless flow of data across agencies.

With the advent of the single window customs processing system for the TFTA we should begin to see an overall improvement in trade indicators across the region through improved customs clearance times, less time spent at border crossings, increase in revenue collections, more accurate statistics of trade inflows and outflows across the region and less leakage of revenue due to corruption at borders. Traders will also enjoy access to a comprehensive customs information portal constructed to satisfy specific customs needs and requirements. This portal would also contain information about rules on the movement of goods across borders, other than customs legislation and would also offer practical customs information for the movement of cargo and its customs treatment.[254]

---

[254] Electronic Customs Multi-Annual Strategic Plan: 2008 Yearly Revision (MASP) European Commission Directorate-General Taxation and Customs Union available at *http://ec.europa.eu/taxation_customs/resources/documents/customs/policy_issues/e-customs_initiative/MASP_strategic_plan_en.pdf* (accessed 20 April 2013).

Despite the challenges which will inevitably crop up in this regional project, there is hope yet in the achievement of the aforementioned goals towards the creation of a regional economic community which is set to become a lucrative destination for international investment through the creation of an enabling investment climate which fosters free trade and easier movement of business persons. To add to this, the adoption of a regional customs protocol which will inform relevant national legislation will demand the reconciliation of national and regional interests of member states and the balancing of national political interests which will be able to cater for necessary subsequent changes. These interests as enumerated above and in previous parts of this thesis may well entail a relatively substantial loss of sovereignty over national trade policy instruments and revenue sources in the short term but will begin to yield strong gains in the long run.[255] This level of integration will then begin to yield positive and sustainable economic returns on a regional investment in modernisation and harmonisation of customs legislation by the TFTA.

This mini-thesis is approximately 33 398 words in length (chapters and footnotes excluding bibliography).

[255] Chauffour J and Maur J (eds) *Preferential Trade Agreement Policies for Development: A Handbook*, edited by Jean-Pierre (2011) 111-2.

BIBLIOGRAPHY

A. PRINTED SOURCES

ARTICLES

Maitland C and Van Gorp, 'Beyond Harmonization: ICT Policymaking in Regional Economic Communities', *Information Society*, (2009).

Wilson J, et al *'Assessing the Benefits of Trade Facilitation: A Global Perspective' The World Bank, Institute for International Economics, Washington DC, and Osaka University, Japan.*

BOOKS

Chauffour J and Maur J (eds) *Preferential Trade Agreement Policies for Development: A Handbook*, edited by Jean-Pierre (2011) The World Bank, Washington D.C.

Clapham C, Mills G, et al '*Regional Integration in South Africa: Comparative International Perspectives'* (2001) South African Institute of International Affairs, Natal Witness.

De Wulf .L and Sokol J.B *Customs Modernization Handbook* (2005) The World Bank, Washington D.C.

Hartzenberg T et al *The Tripartite Free Trade Area – Towards a new African Integration Paradigm?* (2012) Trade Law Centre, RSAM Printers, Kuils River.

Hoekman B, et al (eds) *Development, Trade, and the WTO: A Handbook* (2002) The World Bank, Washington D.C.

Lakshmanan T et al, *Integration of Transport and Trade Facilitation Selected Regional Case Studies,* (2011) The World Bank, Washington D.C.

Lasok D, *The trade and customs law of the European Union* (1998) Kluwer Law International, London.

McLinden .G et al *Border Management Modernisation* (2011) The World Bank, Washington D.C.

Pietrzyk M, *International order and individual liberty: Effects of war and peace on the development of governments* (2002) University Press of America, Maryland.

Schiff M and Winters A. L, *Regional integration and development* (2003) World Bank and Oxford University Press.

Urwin D, *Community of Europe: A history of European Integration since 1945* (1995) Longman, London and New York.

TREATIES AND CONVENTIONS

Abuja Treaty, 1991.

Agreement to establish and implement the ASEAN single window, Kuala Lumpur, 2005.

Arusha Declaration on Customs integrity, 1993.

Convention Relating to Temporary Admission (Istanbul Convention) 1990.

Draft Agreement Establishing the COMESA-EAC-SADC Tripartite Free Trade Area, 2010.

International Convention on Mutual Administrative Assistance for the Prevention, Investigation and Repression of Customs Offences, 1977.

International Convention on the Simplification and Harmonisation of Customs Procedures, Kyoto,1973

Revised International Convention on Mutual Administrative Assistance for the Prevention, Investigation and Repression of Customs Offences, 2003.

Single European Act (SEA), 1986.

Treaty establishing the European Coal and Steel Community, 1951.

Treaty establishing the European Economic Community (Treaty of Rome) 1957.

Treaty on European Union (Maastricht Treaty) 1992.

B. ELECTRONIC SOURCES

JOURNAL ARTICLES

Kieck E, 'Coordinated Border Management: Unlocking trade opportunities through One Stop Border Posts' (2010) 4 *WCJ* 7 available at *http://worldcustomsjournal.org/media/wcj/-2010/1/Kieck.pdf* (accessed 4 May 2013).

Messerlin P, Zarouk J, 'Trade Facilitation: Technical regulations and customs procedures', *World Economy* 23, (2000) Vol. 4 584-587.

Otieno L. and Shinyekwa I 'Prospects and challenges in the formation of the COMESA-EAC-SADC Tripartite Free Trade Area' *Research Series 87 Economic Policy Research Centre* Nov. 2011 available at *http://www.eprc.or.ug/pdf_files/series87.pdf* (accessed 4 May 2013).

Puggliatti L, 'Cloud single window: legal implications of a new model of cross-border single window' (2011) 5 *WCJ* 13 available at *http://www.worldcustomsjournal.org/media/wcj/-2011/2/Pugliatti.pdf* (accessed 4 May 2013).

Shayanowako P, 'Towards a Tripartite Free Trade Area' *Trade and development studies* Issue No. 40 (2011) available at *http://www.panafricanglobaltradeconference.com/upload/towards_a_tripartite_free_trade_area_.pdf* (accessed 4 May 2013).

Thirlwall A and Hussain M, 'The Balance of payments constraint, capital flows and growth rate, differences between developing countries' *Oxford Economic Papers, New Series* (1982) 34, 498-510 at 500 available at *http://down.cenet.org.cn/upfile/94/200512382736170.pdf* (accessed 3 April 2013).

LEGISLATION AND REGULATIONS

EC Commission regulation 2286/2003 of 18 December 2003 available at *http://eur-lex.europa.eu/LexUriServ/LexUriServ.do?uri=OJ:L:2003:343:0001:0123:en:PDF* (accessed 4 May 2013).

EC Commission regulation 2913/92 of 12 October 1992 establishing the community customs code available at *http://eur-lex.europa.eu/LexUriServ/LexUriServ.do?uri=CELEX:31992R2913:en:HTML* (accessed 4 May 2013).

EC Commission regulation 450/2008 of the European Parliament and of the Council of 23 April 2008 laying down the Community Customs Code available at *http://eur-lex.europa.eu/LexUriServ/LexUriServ.do?uri=OJ:L:2008:145:0001:0064:En:PDF* (accessed 4 May 2013).

EC Commission Regulation 648/2005 of the European Parliament and of the Council amending Council Regulation (EEC) No 2913/92; available at *http://eur-lex.europa.eu/LexUriServ/LexUriServ.do?uri=CELEX:32005R0648:en:HTML*

WORKING PAPERS

Andrew Grainger 'Trade Facilitation: A Review' *Trade Facilitation Working Paper* 25 June 2007 available at *www.tradefacilitation.co.uk* (accessed 3 April 2013).

Dobronogov. A & Farole T 'An Economic Integration Zone for the East African Community Exploiting Regional Potential and Addressing Commitment Challenges' *Policy Research Working Paper* No. 5967 World Bank Africa Region Poverty Reduction and Economic Management Unit (2012) 5 available at *http://www-wds.worldbank.org/external/default/WDSContentServer/WDSP/IB/2012/02/13/000158349_20120213133305/Rendered/INDEX/WPS5967.txt* (accessed 20 April 2013).

Engman M, O. Onodera and E. Pinali, 'Export Processing Zones: Past and Future Role in Trade and Development', *OECD Trade Policy Working Papers* (2007) No. 53 available at http://dx.doi.org/10.1787/035168776831 (accessed 4 May 2013).

Evans D 'Options for Regional Integration in Southern Africa' *IDS Working Paper* 94 7 available at *http://acp-eu-trade.org/library/files/EVANS_IDS_wp94_2001_options%20for%20RI%20in%20Sthn%20Africa.pdf* (accessed 25 April 2013).

Hartzenberg T 'Regional Integration in Africa' *Staff Working Paper ERSD*-2011-14, WTO Economic Research and Statistics Division (2011) available at *http://www.wto.org/english/res_e/reser_e/ersd201114_e.pdf* (accessed 25 April 2013).

The 1996 Single Market Review 'Background Information for the Report to the Council' *EU Commission staff working paper* available at *http://ec.europa.eu/internal_market/economic-reports/docs/bkground_en.pdf* (accessed 4 May 2013).

Zake J, 'Customs reform and Modernization in Anglophone Africa Early 1990s to mid 2010' *IMF working paper* WP11/184 available at *http://www.imf.org/external/pubs/ft/wp/2011/wp11184.pdf* (accessed 3 April 2013).

DISCUSSION PAPERS AND SPEECHES

Apostolov M, 'The Single Window and data harmonization in line with international standards' 7th Meeting of the CAREC Customs Cooperation Committee Issy-Kul, 8-9 Sept.2008 available at http://www.carecprogram.org/uploads/events/2008/7th-CCC/UNECE-Single-Window-Data-Harmonization.pdf (accessed 4 May 2013).

Butterly T, 'UNECE Recommendations, Standards and tools for International Trade Single Window' *United Nations Economic Commission for Europe (UNECE)* available at *http://css.escwa.org.lb/edgd/1476/d1s1-2.pdf* (accessed 4 April 2013).

Chaitezvi C *Trade Facilitation in Eastern and Southern Africa: WTO Trade Facilitation Symposium, Geneva 2012* available at *https://www.wto.org/english/tratop_e/tradfa_e/case_studies_e/session6_trademark_e.ppt*. (accessed 4 May 2013).

David J, *ASYCUDA - A recommended IT system for a Customs-centric Single Window and Interconnectivity*
UNCTAD Presentation at Casablanca, February 2013 available at *http://www.itfc-idb.org/files/UNCTAD-ASYCUDA.pdf* (accessed 3 April 2013).

Disenyana, Tsidiso, 'Towards an EAC, COMESA and SADC Free Trade Area: Issues and Challenges.' *SAIIA Discussion Paper* available at *http://www.afdb.org/fileadmin/uploads/afdb/Documents/Knowledge/2009%20AEC-%20Towards%20an%20EAC%20COMESA%20and%20SADC%20Free%20Trade%20Area%20Issues%20and%20Challenges.pdf*. (accessed 4 May 2013).

Duval Y, 'Legal Issues and Cross-Border Paperless Trade Facilitation' *ESCAP Work Programme on Electronic Single Window*, available at *http://www.unescap.org/idd/events/2012-Colombo-meeting/6-1-Mr-Yann-D.pdf* (accessed 18 April 2013).

Kingombe C 'Lessons Learned from the Tripartite Free Trade Area' NEPAD Regional Integration and Trade Department (ONRI) African Development Bank Expert Group meeting on Preferential Trade Agreements and Regional Integration 5 December 2012 available at *http://www.academia.edu/2243183/Lessons_Learned_from_the_Tripartite-Free_Trade_Area* (accessed 4 May 2013).

Koh Tat Tsen. J *Single Windows and Supply Chains in the Next Decade, ten years of single window implementation: lessons learned for the future* Discussion paper Global Trade Facilitation Conference (2011) available at *http://www.unece.org/fileadmin/DAM/trade/Trade_Facilitation_Forum/BkgrdDocs/TenYearsSingleWindow.pdf* (accessed 4 May 2013).

Koh Tat Tsen J 'Single Windows in developing countries: Sharing experiences and lessons learnt from countries in the region and region initiatives' ESCAP-ECO Joint Trade Facilitation Forum on paperless trade and single window, 25-25 May (2012) available at *http://www.unescap.org/tid/projects/swiran-s6koh.pdf* (accessed 18 April 2013).

Luddy W *ASEAN Single window: The intersection of law and technology* Paper presented to ASEAN Secretariat (2008) 17 available at *http://pdf.usaid.gov/pdf_docs/PNADM816.pdf* accessed 3 April 2013).

Luddy W. 'Single Window and Paperless Trade Legal Issues: A Possible Mosaic' Global Trade Facilitation Conference 2011 available at http://www.unece.org/fileadmin/DAM/trade/Trade_Facilitation_Forum/ConferencePPTs/D02_08AM_BillLuddy.pdf. (accessed 4 April 2013).

Mongelli F et al, 'What does European institutional integration tell us about trade integration?' *Occasional Paper Series No. 40* (2005) European Central Bank available at http://www.ecb.int/pub/pdf/scpops/ecbocp40.pdf (accessed 4 May 2013).

Nhara A 'Towards a Tripartite COMESA – EAC – SADC Free Trade Area: A panacea for deeper regional integration or a rhetoric African grouping' Trade and Development Studies Centre (2011) available at http://cloud2.gdnet.org/cms.php?id=research_paper_abstract&research_paper_id=18275 (accessed 4 May 2013).

Pearson M, 'Trade Facilitation in the COMESA-EAC-SADC Tripartite Free Trade Area' September 2011 available at http://www.trademarksa.org/publications/trade-facilitation-comesa-eac-sadc-tripartite-free-trade-area (accessed 4 May 2013).

Ponten J, 'Single window – best practice and the way forward' Discussion paper *UNCITRAL colloquium on electronic commerce* New York, USA, February 14-16th 2011 available at http://www.uncitral.org/pdf/english/colloquia/EC/Ponten_SW_Best_Practice_and_the_Way_Forward.pdf (accessed 4 May 2013).

Southern Africa Regional Integration strategy paper 2011 – 2015 *African Development Bank* http://www.afdb.org/fileadmin/uploads/afdb/Documents/Project-and-Operations/2011-2015%20-%20Southern%20Africa%20-%20Regional%20Integration%20Strategy%20Paper.pdf (accessed 4 May 2013).

POLICY BRIEFS AND NOTES

Rippel B 'Why Trade Facilitation is Important for Africa' *Africa Trade Policy Notes, 27*, World Bank (2011) available at http://siteresources.worldbank.org/INTAFRREGTOPTRADE/Resources/trade_facilitation_note_nov11.pdf (accessed 4 May 2013).

'The costs and benefits of trade facilitation' *OECD Policy Brief* October 2005 available at http://www.mincomes.it/semproitalia/tavolo_strategico/8_documenti/OCSE/OCSE/Contenuti/Cost%20Benefits%20of%20Trade%20Facilitation.pdf (accessed 4 May 2013).

Towards a single window trading environment 'Achieving effective stakeholder coordination' *United Nations Network of Experts for paperless trade in Asia and the Pacific* Brief no.7 September 2011 available at http://www.unescap.org/unnext/pub/brief7.pdf (accessed 3 April 2013).

REPORTS

Prechal S. & De Leeuw E, '*General Principles of EC Law in A Process of Development: Reports from A Conference in Stockholm*' 202. Available at http://www.uu.nl/faculty/leg/NL/organisatie/departementen/departementrechtsgeleerdheid/organisatie/onderdelen/europainstituut/publicaties/algemenerechtsbeginselen/Documents/S.%20Prechal%20en%20M.E.%20de%20Leeuw,%20Transparancy.pdf (accessed 25 April 2013).

Report of the first Tripartite technical meeting on standards harmonisation, 2010 Pretoria available at http://www.trademarksa.org/sites/default/files/publications/REPORT%20OF%201ST%20TRIPAR

TITE%20TECH%20MEETING%20ON%20STANDARDS%20HARMONIZATION(final).pdf (accessed 4 May 2013).

Report of the Tripartite OSBP Workshop, 2011 Johannesburg, South Africa available at *http://tis.sadc.int/files/4813/3068/3347/Report_-_Regional_OSBP_Workshop_2627_Oct_11_Johannesburg.pdf* (accessed 4 May 2013).

Technical Report: Audit of the Implementation of Regional SADC Customs Instruments and International Conventions Southern African Trade Hub October 2011 available at *http://www.satradehub.org/trade-facilitation/2011-audit-of-the-implementation-of-regional-sadc-customs-instruments-and-international-conventions/callelement*. (accessed 4 May 2013).

WTO DOCUMENTS

Doha development agenda: Doha Work programme WTO available at *http://www.wto.org/english/tratop_e/dda_e/draft_text_gc_dg_31july04_e.htm* (accessed 3 April 2013).

Experience on the Development of the ASEAN Single Window Negotiating Group on Trade Facilitation TN/TF/W/105 WTO Communication from ASEAN available at *http://www.wcoomd.org/en/topics/facilitation/activities-and-programmes/wto-trade-facilitation-negotiations/~/media/131F8CBF311E4EDC92FFA774F64B2D28.ashx* (accessed 4 April 2013).

Key Factors in Establishing Single Windows for Handling Import/Export Procedures and Formalities: Trade Facilitation and the Single Window E/ESCWA/EDGD/2011/5 10 November 2011 at 27 available at *http://www.wto.org/english/tratop_e/tradfa_e/case_studies_e/escwa_e.pdf* (accessed 3 April 2013).

Trade facilitation case study on customs cooperation between Zambia and Zimbabwe. Presented at the World Trade Organisation Symposium November 2011 Geneva available at *https://www.wto.org/english/tratop_e/tradfa_e/case_studies_e/bac_zmb_e.doc* (accessed 4 May 2013).

'Trade policies and practices by measure' WTO Trade Policy Review available at *http://www.wto.org/english/tratop_e/tpr_e/s214-03_e.doc* (accessed 4 May 2013).

WTO Briefing notes on Doha agenda and trade facilitation available at *http://www.wto.org/english/tratop_e/dda_e/status_e/tradfa_e.htm* (accessed 3 April 2013).

EU COMMUNICATIONS AND DOCUMENTS

Borchardt K, 'The ABC of European Union law' *EU* (2010) available at *http://europa.eu/documentation/legislation/pdf/oa8107147_en.pdf* (accessed 4 May 2013).

COM/2003/452 of 24/07/2003 A simple and paperless environment for customs and trade available at *http://ec.europa.eu/prelex/detail_dossier_real.cfm?CL=en&DosId=184452* (accessed 4 May 2013).

Communication from the Commission to the Council, the European Parliament and the European Economic and Social Committee Strategy for the evolution of the customs union. Com (2008) 169_en) available at *http://ec.europa.eu/taxation_customs/resources/documents/customs/com(2008)169_en.pdf* (accessed 4 May 2013).

Communication from the Commission to the Council, the European Parliament and the European Economic and social committee on the state of the customs union Brussels (2012) available at *http://ec.europa.eu/taxation_customs/resources/documents/common/publications/com_reports/customs/com(2012)791_en.pdf* (accessed 4 May 2013).

DG Taxation and Customs Union Management Plan 2012 available at *http://ec.europa.eu/atwork/synthesis/amp/doc/taxud_mp.pdf* (accessed 4 May 2013).

Electronic Customs Multi-Annual Strategic Plan: 2008 Yearly Revision (MASP) European Commission Directorate-General Taxation and Customs Union available at *http://ec.europa.eu/taxation_customs/resources/documents/customs/policy_issues/e-customs_initiative/MASP_strategic_plan_en.pdf* (accessed 20 April 2013).

European Commission: Taxation and Customs Union-Electronic_customs_initiative It_projects available at *http://ec.europa.eu/taxation_customs/customs/policy_issues/electronic_customs_initiative/it_projects/* (last accessed 21 April 2013).

Economic Commission for Europe: The Single Window Concept available at *http://unpan1.un.org/intradoc/groups/public/documents/UNECE/UNPAN019892.pdf* (accessed 4 May 2013).

Fontaine P. *Europe in 12 lessons* European Commission (2006) available at *http://ec.europa.eu/archives/publications/booklets/eu_glance/60/en.pdf* (accessed 4 May 2013).

'New customs transit systems for Europe' prepared by the office for official publications of the European Communities (2001) available at *http://ec.europa.eu/taxation_customs/resources/documents/annex_i_transit_brochure_en.pdf* (accessed 4 May 2013).

'The single administrative document' European Commission: Taxation and Customs Union available at *http://ec.europa.eu/taxation_customs/customs/procedural_aspects/general/sad/* (accessed 4 May 2013).

NEWSPAPER ARTICLES

Muwanga D, 'COMESA, SADC, EAC talks overdue' East African Business Week Monday, February 18th, 2013 available at *http://www.busiweek.com/index.php/the-eac-issues/eac-news/4517-comesa-sadc-eac-talks-overdue-* (accessed 4 May 2013).

WCO: 'There is strong commitment to customs modernisation in Africa' *All Africa.com* 14 March 2012 available at *http://allafrica.com/stories/201203141063.html* (accessed 4 May 2013).

National single window facilitates trade in the Philippines. *http://www.crownagents.com/national-single-window-facilitates-trade-in-the-philippines.aspx* (accessed 4 May 2013).

NRA/BURS – Customs connectivity passes test: What happened to the Portcullis? Available at http://mpoverello.com/2013/01/24/namburs-customs-connectivity-passes-test/ (accessed 4 May 2013).

UNCTAD TECHNICAL NOTES

UNCTAD Trust Fund for Trade Facilitation Negotiations Technical Note No. 3 Use of Customs automated systems available at *http://r0.unctad.org/ttl/technical-notes/TN03_CustomsAutomationSystems.pdf* (accessed 4 May 2013).

UNCTAD Trust Fund for trade facilitation negotiations technical note 13 available at *http://www.unctad.org/technicalnotes* (accessed 4 May 2013).

UNCTAD Trust Fund for Trade Facilitation negotiations Technical Note No. 21 ASYCUDA available at *http://unctad.org/en/docs/TN21_Asycuda.pdf* (accessed 4 May 2013).

OTHER ORGANISATIONAL WEBSITES

Aid for Trade Global Review: Microsoft and the Trans-Kalahari Corridor Regional Single Window available at http://www.oecd.org/aidfortrade/48367286.pdf (accessed 4 May 2013).

Aid For Trade Case Story - The COMESA-EAC-SADC Tripartite Trade and Transport Facilitation Programme available at *http://www.oecd.org/aidfortrade/47407250.pdf* (accessed 4 May 2013).

Aid for trade case story: Zimbabwe-Chirundu One Stop Border Post, A Regional Trade Facilitation Programme available at http://www.oecd.org/aidfortrade/47750237.pdf (accessed 4 May 2013).

ASYCUDA in Africa information sheet AW-IS/MP/AF 25 available at *http://www.unctadxi.org/sections/wsis/docs/asycuda/AW-IS-MP-AF-v4_en.pdf* (accessed 3 April 2013).

Benefits of ASYCUDA World available at *http://www.asycuda.org/awbenefits.asp* (accessed 4 May 2013).

COMESA Customs Union: Brief on the COMESA Customs Union available at *http://programmes.comesa.int/index.php?option=com_content&view=article&id=90&Itemid=142* (accessed 4 May 2013).

COMESA-EAC-SADC Tripartite - institutional framework available at *http://www.comesa-eac-TFTA-tripartite.org/home* (accessed 4 May 2013).

Ganz R, Hallstein Notes Political Goals of Common Market available at, *http://www.thecrimson.com/article/1961/5/23/hallstein-notes-political-goals-of-common/* (accessed 4 May 2013).

Kyoto Convention guidelines on the application of information and communication technology by the World Customs Organisation June 2004 at 16 available at *http://www.insw.go.id/images/public/kyoto-ict-guidelines-wco.pdf* (accessed 3 April 2013).

Logistic Performance Index, World Bank available at *http://web.worldbank.org/WBSITE/EXTERNAL/TOPICS/EXTTRANSPORT/EXTTLF/0,,contentMDK:21514122~menuPK:3875957~pagePK:210058~piPK:210062~theSitePK:515434,00.html* (accessed 4 May 2013).

Recommendation 33 – *Recommendation and Guidelines on Establishing a Single Window*, July 2005, United Nations Centre for Trade Facilitation and Electronic Business UNCEFACT (2005) available at *www.unece.org/cefact/recommendations/rec35/Rec35-PublicReviewDraftv9-Feb09.doc* (accessed 3 April 2013)

Recommendation 35 – *Establishing a legal framework for international trade Single Window*, October 2010, UNCEFACT (2010) available at *www.unece.org/cefact/recommendations/rec35/Rec35-PublicReviewDraftv9-Feb09.doc* (accessed 3 April 2013).

SADC and the African Union - Tripartite Cooperation available at *http://www.sadc.int/about-sadc/continental-interregional-integration/tripartite-cooperation/* (accessed 4 May 2013).

SADC Draft guidelines for coordinated border management available at *http://www.trademarksa.org/sites/default/files/publications/Guidelines%20%7C%20Draft%20SADC%20guidelines%20for%20Coordinated%20Border%20Management%20%7C%20A%20Practical%20Guide%20on%20Best%20Practices%20and%20Tools%20for%20Implementation.pdf* (accessed 4 May 2013).

Southern African Trade Hub – Regional Customs Connectivity Customs pilot programme available at *http://www.satradehub.org/customs-connectivity/sath-content/activities/trade-facilitation/customs-connectivity* (accessed 4 May 2013).

TradeMark South Africa available at *http://www.trademarksa.org/node/1042* (accessed 4 May 2013).

Trading across borders, doing business-the World Bank Group available at *http://www.doingbusiness.org/data/exploretopics/trading-across-borders* (accessed 4 May 2013).

Walter Hallstein EU Commission President from 1958 to 1967 available at *http://www4.dr-rath-foundation.org/brussels_eu/who_is_who/index.html* (accessed 4 May 2013).

What is the European Union? Available at *http://eeas.europa.eu/delegations/new_zealand/eu_new_zealand/political_economics_relations/agreements/faq/index_en.htm* (last accessed 13 March 2013).

World Customs Organisation data model, Single window data harmonisation available at *http://www.mincomes.it/semproitalia/tavolo_strategico/8_documenti/WCO/Documenti/WCO_Data%20Model_for_SW.pdf* (accessed 4 May 2013).

WCO Data Model Connects trade stakeholders available at *http://www.wcoomd.org/en/topics/facilitation/resources/~/media/3267E6020CA044359C1B479F6515A93F.ashx* (accessed 4 May 2013).